BART VS. MY HOPES & DREAMS

Looking Back at Thirty Years of Video Games
Based on *The Simpsons*

The Unauthorized Retrospective
by Victor Romero

First Release: itch.io, 2021

Second Release: Print, 2024

Table of Contents

Introduction: The Caveats

When I started writing this book I knew one person wanted it to exist, and baby, you're looking at him... in your mind... as you read. Do I look alright? Pick a nice outfit for me.

As you'll discover during the course of this retrospective, I became weirdly fascinated with video games based on *The Simpsons*, and all I ever really wanted was a central repository of information about them. Some of these video games were seldom discussed online and I was left to discover much of what I know on my own by scouring eBay, the GameFAQs database, and plenty of long-lost online sources. I eventually compiled what I knew on my own fan website and in the myriad walkthroughs that I wrote over the years. That was enough... for a time. Then I saw that there was a place in the world for super niche books and I realized there was exactly one super niche topic I should write a book about.

Part of my decision to write the book came from the fact that I instantly imagined the structure of the whole thing. Each video game would get its own chapter, and each chapter required similar key beats. This meant that I would tread the same territory that many others have trod for certain popular or infamous titles, but my favorite part was expanding upon the history and details of those *Simpsons* video games that rarely get more than a passing glance. That includes my personal background with the games, developer history, an overview of the story (as it is) and gameplay, and even some release data such as the month and year in which they were released. I accrued all this information by poring over sources from both the Internet and the analog world of books and magazines, and I tried to be as accurate as possible. I've often thought that a work's existence justifies its documentation and analysis, and it just takes a particular weirdo to take the time to do it. Ahem.

Some readers may peruse this book's contents and think "Wait, where's *The Simpsons Cartoon Studio?*" or "What about those handheld games from Tiger Electronics?" or even "there's also a VR app!" Those things are cool and certainly a part of the larger story of merchandise and media based on *The Simpsons*, but I made the decision to focus on the video games, meaning those electronic games which are played on video screens and are designed as distinctly interactive experiences with meaningful gameplay and goals. I have no qualms about leaving out *The Simpsons Cartoon Studio* as it is clearly a media creation app, and those handheld LCD games are interesting but not really *video* games. The aforementioned "Planet of the Couches" VR app from 2016 (described by its creators as a couch gag in virtual reality) is rad but... is it a video game? One might say that if I include *Virtual Springfield* then I should include "Planet of the Couches" as well, but I found the VR app just didn't reach my threshold of "meaningful" interactivity. The Simpsons have even appeared in *Minecraft* and *Lego Dimensions*, but only as cameos and DLC. Look, it's all arbitrary! Maybe my acute case of Simpsonsmania will bring me back around for another book about the even lesser known *Simpsons* electronic games and interactive experiences. There are so many!

God. There are... so... many.

So, uh, enjoy reading about a whole bunch of them.

Chapter 1: The Quarter Muncher

The Simpsons Arcade Game - December 1990

When I think of *The Simpsons* arcade game, I think of purple hippo trash cans. These terrifying monoliths were the favored receptacle at the video arcade in the main plaza of the city of Tepatitlán, Jalisco. The video arcade was a wonderland of animal-shaped architecture, the smell of fried chips doused in hot sauce and lemon sold at the front counter, and even an old ball pit that would see an occasional and exceptionally brave visitor dive into its depths.

But the main draw, the reason we spent our parents' hard-earned pesos there, was the arcade games that lined the walls. You may be familiar with some of them. The wild west shoot 'em up of *Sunset Riders*, time-traveling brawlers in *World Heroes*, and even brutal gun cabinets like *Lethal Enforcers*. And far in the back corner was *The Simpsons*. We'd play other games, but to me, that was the crown jewel of the joint.

I had seen *The Simpsons* arcade game before, though never in the glow of an American video arcade. Such places were deemed a waste of quarters by my parents. I'd see the game in a swapmeet cafeteria, or in the back corner of a gas station. And frankly, I could never hope to have enough quarters to get very far in the game. But in

Mexico, in that little arcade in the plaza, the American dollar went far. So it came to pass that I, my brothers, and our cousins came together to tackle the game with all the tokens we could ever dream of. It was my first time actually reaching the finale until the wonders of arcade emulation brought the arcade game back into my life many years later. As a fan of *The Simpsons* and video games, it was always on my mind.

Choose your nuclear family.

It is woefully inadequate to call *The Simpsons* a phenomenon. The show—developed by *Life in Hell* cartoonist Matt Groening and producer James L. Brooks's Gracie Films—started as a series of interstitial animated shorts on *The Tracey Ullman Show*. The shorts quickly

8

outgrew Ullman's variety show and premiered as an animated sitcom of their own. The subversive humor, dysfunctional family dynamics, and bizarre character designs took the world by storm, blowing up immediately after the premiere on the Fox Television network on December 17, 1989.

The popularity brought a level of success that demanded more than just revenue from television advertising. The savvy heads of merchandising at Fox knew a cash cow when they saw one. As the chairman of Fox reportedly told his vice president of licensing and marketing, "The show will debut on January 14—go to work".[1] And work they did, signing deals wherever the money was available. Groening himself was also eager to see his creations licensed as widely as possible, with final approval on all products running through him and Gracie Films. Merchandising revenues were estimated to be upwards of $750 million by the end of 1990.[2]

It was in the middle of this merchandising frenzy that Fox signed multiple deals to release video games based on *The Simpsons*. The companies developing electronic games from the license in the first years included handheld game manufacturer Tiger Electronics; game publisher Acclaim Entertainment (we'll dive into their catalog in later chapters); and Konami, the renowned powerhouse known for its high-quality and highly profitable hits both in arcades and on home consoles such as the Nintendo

Entertainment System. It was Konami that would develop the first game (and what many fans consider to be the best game) based on *The Simpsons* ever made: *The Simpsons* arcade game.

FLASHBACK
ARCADE GAME HISTORY

DEVELOPMENT TIMELINE

THE SIMPSONS™ ARCADE GAME WAS THE FIRST SIMPSONS VIDEO GAME EVER MADE.

FEBRUARY 26, 1990 DEVELOPMENT STARTED ON THE SIMPSONS™ ARCADE GAME.

DECEMBER 17, 1990 A LOCATION TEST WAS PERFORMED IN CHICAGO, ILLINOIS, WITH THE GAME'S FIRST ARCADE CABINET.

JANUARY 21, 1991 A SECOND LOCATION TEST WAS PERFORMED IN THE SAME CITY.

FEBRUARY 28, 1991 MASS PRODUCTION OF THE ARCADE GAME WAS COMPLETE.

MARCH 12, 1991 THE U.S. VERSION WAS OFFICIALLY RELEASED.

AUGUST 21, 1991 THE JAPANESE VERSION WAS RELEASED FIVE MONTHS LATER.

A BRIEF HISTORY FOR THE FANS

Konami comes on strong.

According to the official timeline from Konami, development of the game began in February 1990, a little over one month after the Christmas-themed episode "Simpsons Roasting on an Open Fire" kicked off the standalone series. The executives at Fox couldn't have chosen a better partner to develop an arcade game. Based in Kobe, Japan, Konami had grown to be a juggernaut of the video game industry based on the success of games like stealth action game *Metal Gear*, space shooter *Gradius*, and other licensed games such as *Teenage Mutant Ninja*

Turtles, or *TMNT* for short.[3] These games weren't just profitable, they were fun! Although *The Simpsons* television show and characters wouldn't be familiar to Japanese television viewers until years later (and even today are primarily known as advertising mascots for a soft drink called CC Lemon[4]), it was the Japanese developers at Konami who were tasked with creating the first arcade game using only a few months' worth of scripts, animation, and character information. Armed with top-notch designers and hardware that no console or home computer could match, the team was off on the right track.

The developers settled on a core concept for the gameplay: a brawler game, with a joystick for movement, one button for attacks, and another button for jumping. The aforementioned *TMNT* arcade game was a similar brawler released in 1989 that captured the essence and art style of the license perfectly, and its four-player configuration transposed nicely to the core cast of the *The Simpsons*: oafish Homer, bratty Bart, studious Lisa, and industrious Marge. Maggie, the baby of the family, would serve the same role as the "princess in another castle" from the *Super Mario Bros.* series, in which the object of Mario's affection is repeatedly yanked away just as he is on the verge of rescuing her. It may seem strange for a sitcom family to become brawling vigilantes, but the exaggeration is simply part of the animated show's ability to "elastically expand," like the surreal and reality-breaking "Treehouse of Horror" episodes, or anthology episodes of biblical and literary stories featuring characters from the show.[5] This elasticity will apply to the ever-wackier premises and antics in future video games based on *The Simpsons*.

It is interesting that although there is a lineage of brawler games at Konami before *The Simpsons* arcade game, few of the staff on *The Simpsons* development team had experience with the genre before the project, and fewer still went on to work on more brawler games, with just a handful going on to work on the notable sequel to *TMNT* and a *Bucky O'Hare* game in 1992, and a *X-Men* game in 1993. The shift was likely a response to the burgeoning fighting game genre after the release of Capcom's *Street Fighter II* in 1991, but one has to wonder if working on strange and cartoonish Western properties had lost its appeal for Japanese developers. *The Simpsons* arcade game would be the only game based on *The Simpsons* television show to be created by a company based in Japan until Konami's return to the license a decade later.

The family that brawls together.

The premise is refreshingly simple. The Simpson family is out on a stroll through their hometown of Springfield when they literally bump into Waylon Smithers—lackey of the nuclear power magnate, C. Montgomery Burns—just as he flees a jewelry store with a diamond the size of a pacifier. The diamond flies into the air, lands in Maggie's mouth, and the only sensible thing for Smithers to do is take back the diamond, baby and all.

With the excuse for clobbering goons out of the way, players are free to select their Simpson and go to town. Each character has their own unique abilities. Homer's fighting style involves the most standard of brawler weapons: his fists. This limits the character's range and makes his attacks the most visceral, going head-to-head with the legions of goons in his trademark "kick some back" style.[6] Next on the character selection screen is Bart, who rides his skateboard and wields it like a street skater from the nineties out for blood. Lisa's weapon is her jump rope, which I suppose is more respectful than using an expensive saxophone to bash heads. And finally there's Marge, whose role as the homemaker justifies her use of a full-on vacuum cleaner to strike foes in the gut. Personally, I appreciate Marge's reach with that vacuum cleaner and always select her, much like choosing Donatello with his extended bo staff in the *TMNT* games. The characters can even team up to perform special tag team attacks: Homer and Marge roll around in a marital wheel, Bart and Lisa hold hands to clothesline enemies, Homer can pick up the kids on his shoulder for double firepower, and Marge can toss them for a powerful projectile attack. As the earliest video game, *The Simpsons* arcade game was created before "Bartmania" took hold of Americans' minds and wallets.[7] As such, each character enjoyed equal billing. It made for a holistic experience in which the entire family plays a prominent role in being the hero of the story.

Cartoonishly brutal as they are, both the Simpsons and their foes are all impressively animated, with dynamic poses and hilariously off-model reactions to the varying attacks. Even doing nothing is a joy by just watching idle animations or waiting for a giant white glove to appear and attack players who fail to move along to the next encounter with enemies. One popular piece of trivia is that some of Marge's animations (her electrocution and the vacuum getting caught in her hair) show a peculiar set of rabbit ears attached to the top of her head, referencing an intended early joke by Matt Groening in which Marge would be revealed to be sporting rabbit ears hidden in her tall hairdo.[8] Such wacky creativity was only possible at the early stage of the show's production when the rules weren't as defined as they would become over the subsequent seasons.

A Smithers for all seasons.

The main villain is the cartoonishly super-villainous Waylon Smithers, sporting a dark cape over his casual business attire and cackling with a hilariously inaccurate voice. He appears at the end of each stage like a dollar tied to a string, pulled along just enough to keep the story moving. When he greets the player with a coarse, whiskey-tinged voice-over reading of "Welcome to my world!," it's the highlight of the eight-level chase to stop him. Sorry, Harry Shearer, but this is my preferred Smithers.

Before that, however, the Simpsons must fight their way through the goon parade. The common goons come in two varieties: suit guy and pink shirts. The suit guys come in a closet's worth of suit colors, with each color indicating the type of attack the goon will perform, such as throwing a hat or simply punching away. The pink shirts, on the other hand, are all identical in appearance and ability, with a bit more health to chip away than the suit guys. The levels are even filled with so many background characters from the show that you may as well check them off a list of characters from the first season. Beyond them are a swath of level-specific enemies such as firefighters, ninjas, and even zombies performing what is undoubtedly the dance from the "Thriller" music video featuring Michael Jackson. The reference may be in poor taste now, but at the time there was no one cooler than Michael Jackson and the Simpsons.[9]

The end-level bosses in the game are all incredibly indulgent in their size and designs. In this *Simpsons* reality, wrestlers and alcoholics can be nine feet tall, and it's totally fine for Mr. Burns to appear inside a mech as the final boss of the game. While none of the bosses are particularly inventive in their attacks (except, perhaps, for the giant bowling ball that serves as the boss of the Dreamland level), they're perfectly suited to face off against a family of brawlers tearing through town.

Wish you were fair.

The Simpsons arcade game presented the first and best version of an interactive Springfield for quite some time. Naturally, most levels were designed after locations from episodes in the first season, including Moe's Tavern, Springfield Butte, Dreamland, Channel 6, and the Springfield Nuclear Power Plant. Moe's Tavern connecting to the Springfield Discount Cemetery via underground bootlegger's passage may seem bizarre, but is it any wackier than the tunnel from the Squidport to Moe's Tavern that appeared later in the series?[10] Other levels were unique creations for the game. Downtown Springfield is your average American Main Street, while Krustyland is a unique creation by the designers at Konami. That Cemetery may have been inspired by early looks at the "Treehouse of Horror" episode that premiered later in 1991. Every locale simply feels cohesive and pieced together naturally. It's a remarkable feat for a team that created the game from concept art and early episodes of the television series.

While the levels look pretty, they're designed to give the player hell. The enemies are relentless and the levels are full of hazards just aching to reduce a player's lives to zero so they are forced to pony up another quarter. This dichotomy between difficulty and fun is the business plan of the video arcade, and unfortunately players of the era were forced to pay up or go home. Players could also strive to achieve high scores if they tired of simply playing through for kicks. Home releases of the game either gave the player enough credits to survive to the end or simply provided infinite credits. Challenge be damned, I'd rather check out all the cool art, gags, and music without breaking the piggy bank.

Lie, cheat, steal, and listen to The Simpsons Arcade music.

And hoo boy, what music. Composer Norio Hanzawa (credited as N. Hanzawa) put together a magnificent soundtrack, with music that riffs on the theme from the television show by Danny Elfman as well as a number of unique compositions just for this game. Hanzawa's work turns away from Alf Clausen's orchestral ditties and instead presents the battlefields of the game with cacophonous chiptune combos that would ill-fit the show but are perfect for a version of *The Simpsons* that doesn't quite fit into the same reality.

The sound effects of the game are equally rich, with bits of dialogue sprinkled throughout to really impress players of an era when voices in a game were still a novelty. The voiced dialogue wasn't going to win any comedy awards, but it's goofy enough and most of the lines are voiced by the actual actors. Those few lines that are clearly not the original actors are so strange that they've become legendary. Smithers's exclamations are one example, but there's also Mr. Burns's raspy threat during the final battle: "Welcome to your grave, suckers." Yep, that's a villain in a mech suit alright.

The beginning of a fraught friendship.

The Simpsons arcade game was released to broad acclaim in North America after location tests in Chicago,

Illinois from December 1990 to January 1991. The game was available in the standard four-player configuration that most players are familiar with, but Konami also released a two-player cabinet, as well as cabinets for other regions such as Japan. Exact revenue numbers are unavailable but the persistent and widespread popularity of the game even today speaks to its quality and the game's legendary status as the best *Simpsons* game ever. It became the bar against which all future games in the series would be measured, and as we'll see in later chapters, many failed to measure up.

The game's legacy cemented what are immutable properties of a good *Simpsons* game:

- The show is built on its ensemble cast of characters. Each member of the family must receive equal time for it to feel like a *Simpsons* game.
- Springfield is a character in and of itself, and all events should transpire within the context of the town. Although the arcade game arrived early in the show's history, its levels are so dense with rich scenery and oddball characters that it feels like a complete world in and of itself.
- Jokes! *The Simpsons* is a television show packed with hilarious dialogue and gags, and while *The Simpsons* arcade game could only squeeze so much dialogue in between the brawling, it is nonetheless rich with sight gags and funny moments, not to mention references,

21

that make it feel like the creators understood what players would expect from a game featuring this world.

Players like me couldn't get enough of the game and after seeing releases of Konami's *TMNT* arcade games on home consoles, we felt certain a home version of *The Simpsons* was close behind. It wasn't until 2012 that console players saw a home version of the game on Xbox 360 and PlayStation 3, but PC players of the early nineties had a couple of options. The game was ported to IBM PC and Commodore 64 computers by a Hungarian company called Novotrade a year after the original arcade launch. The IBM PC version looked amazing for the time and I can easily imagine it playing on a NES or even 16-bit consoles. The Commodore 64 version... Well, it's impressive that they even managed to squeeze the game onto the platform, but it's not the version of the game to play unless you're okay with the Simpsons looking like pixel cyclops.

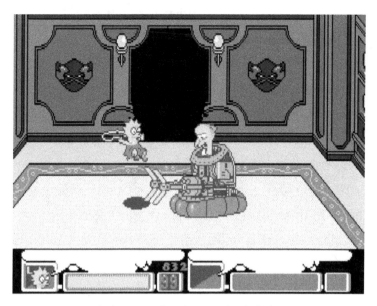

It ain't pretty but it gets the job done.

It's a shame that the game was never ported to home consoles such as the NES where other Konami arcade hits like *TMNT* found great success. This is likely due to Fox's deal with Acclaim Entertainment, which published all console games based on *The Simpsons* for the next several years. At the time it was not unusual for licensing rights to get carved up between different publishers across console, PC, and handheld platforms. This explains Konami's PC publishing with the arcade ports and *Bart's House of Weirdness* (Chapter 5), but nothing on console. Good news: the 2012 releases included uncompromised emulation of the original arcade game, online multiplayer, both USA and Japan ROMs, requisite trophies, and cool extra stuff like a historical timeline of development with key dates. Bad news: these releases were removed from their respective stores just two years later, which allowed those who already owned a copy to retain access to the game but prevented anyone else from purchasing it. It's unclear whether the game will ever be released again but as with all licensing, it comes down to money.

The Simpsons would go on to appear in many video games in this early era of the show, most featuring Bart in a variety of action-platformers. Few would rise to the lofty peaks that arose from this game's crust.

Notes

1. John Ortved, *The Simpsons: An Uncensored, Unauthorized History* (London: Faber and Faber, 2009).
2. Ibid.
3. "A Visit to Konami" (BEEP!, 1987). Translated from the original Japanese by Peter Barnard and archived on shmuplations.com. Retrieved 18 March 2021.
4. "The Simpsons in Japan: A Lesson on Stereotypes" (Tokyo Fox, 2007). Retrieved 18 March 2021.
5. Chris Turner, *Planet Simpson: How a Cartoon Masterpiece Documented an Era and Defined a Generation* (Toronto: Random House Canada, 2004).
6. "Brother from the Same Planet," *The Simpsons* (Fox Television, 1993). Directed by Jeffrey Lynch and written by Jon Vitti.
7. Chris Turner, *Planet Simpson*.

8. John Ortved, *The Simpsons.*

9. Sarah Marsh, "Simpsons producers withdraw Michael Jackson episode" (The Guardian, 2019). Retrieved 18 March 2021.

10. "My Sister, My Sitter," *The Simpsons* (Fox Television, 1997). Directed by Jim Reardon and written by Dan Greaney.

Chapter 2: The Purple Stuff

Bart vs. the Space Mutants - April 1991

This may shock and astound you, but I didn't care for early games based on *The Simpsons*. It may be no coincidence that my first memory of those early games was a brief moment in time with *Bart vs. the Space Mutants*. It was a gloomy, smog-tinted summer afternoon in Los Angeles, California. My mother dragged me along to visit her friend, who had a daughter of my age that was also in my elementary school, though she was in a different classroom and so our social circles were worlds apart. While my mother and her friend chatted, we were left to our own devices. We hung out in her room and she wore the kind of frilly dress that only kids with no control of their lives would wear. We grasped at the straws of childhood conversation until she spoke those magic words: "I have a Nintendo."

She rifled through her older brother's Nintendo cartridges and it was there that I first encountered *Bart vs. the Space Mutants*. I'd seen the character on more T-shirts than there were kids in our school, but a video game was something new. That's the next level of merchandise. We sat on the shag carpet and dove in, goofing around in a first level with way too many objectives for two seven-year olds to enjoy. We tried it for a few minutes before she suggested we go outside and play on the swings in her backyard. We never spoke of that day again.

No, you pay me.

Konami got in early on that *Simpsons* merch parade, but they weren't alone. Although they locked in the *Simpsons* game rights for arcade and PC, an upstart game publisher called Acclaim Entertainment scooped up the rights for home consoles. This process of carving up publishing rights between different groups may seem strange, but it was common at a time when license holders, like, say, a television broadcast company, barely understood the video game industry. It's also likely that publishers hoped to pay less for the licenses by only publishing on specific platforms. It's ultimately not clear why Fox decided to loan the license to different publishers, or if Konami was even offered the opportunity to purchase the home console rights. However, as the book *The Tetris Effect* showed us, it wasn't unusual for publishing rights to become a spaghetti bowl of contracts and agreements.[1] We can be certain that Fox signed whatever deals earned them the most money from *The Simpsons*.

Acclaim itself wasn't yet a developer and they needed to find someone to take on the task. Acclaim may have been founded by former Activision developers, but their business was strictly a publishing affair. Greg Fischbach, vice president at Acclaim, set about acquiring the hot property shortly after it blew up in 1990.[2] Once acquired, he had the task of finding someone to, you know, do the work, and with little time to turn it around. For that we have to go West, young reader, from Acclaim's New York headquarters to the wilds of New Jersey, home of the company that developed the game: Imagineering Inc.

Imagineering was a development subsidiary of an umbrella company called Absolute Entertainment, named so it would be alphabetically listed above competitor Accolade. Both companies were founded by former employees of Activision, which itself was founded by former employees of Atari. Atari, Activision, Accolade, Acclaim, Absolute... my pattern sense is tingling. In any case, Imagineering was presumably created to separate the company's development work from its publishing business, and not to infringe on that other, much more successful Imagineering that works on Disney theme park rides. Imagineering's brief but prolific output includes many a license other than *The Simpsons*, and their volume suggests an aspiration to mediocrity and profit, a goal that likely aligned them well with Acclaim. And this brings us back to the question: how much time did they spend on *Bart vs. the Space Mutants*? One interview with Alex DeMeo, the Vice President/Producer/Game Designer at Absolute Entertainment, suggests that the team may have been trying to churn out games every three or four months, which would explain their prodigious output.[3] However, Garry Kitchen, cofounder of the studio, revealed that it wasn't Imagineering's idea to develop in such a short timeframe.[4]

That's not to detract from Imagineering's ability to create a fun and interesting video game. Its two legendary cofounders, Kitchen and David Crane, built impressive careers in the eighties as designers of fun and successful video games on platforms like the Atari 2600. One of their original and most successful creations at their new company was called *A Boy and His Blob: Trouble on Blobolonia*, and it's easy to see the connection between this game's adventure-oriented level design and the inventive elements of *Bart vs. the Space Mutants*. Kitchen credits designer Barry Marx for recognizing the value of *The Simpsons* and the potential for a great video game.[5]

While their ambition was great, the realities of the schedule settled in quickly. Kitchen recalls, "I think we started July/August. We had to be done by Oct to ship for holidays. We killed ourselves but didn't get Nintendo approval til Dec, shipped Jan. Nintendo was involved (not concept, more mechanic). I didn't want Bart to feel like Mario, they wanted Bart to feel like Mario."[6] So while *The Simpsons* arcade game had nearly a year of development time, Imagineering was saddled with three months at best. This explains the rather rushed feeling of the design in later levels and the overall lack of polish. It was a rough start for what could've been a great game series.

Unfortunately, those shortcomings led other, less inventive elements to dominate the game experience, and those experiences were the stuff of young NES players' nightmares.

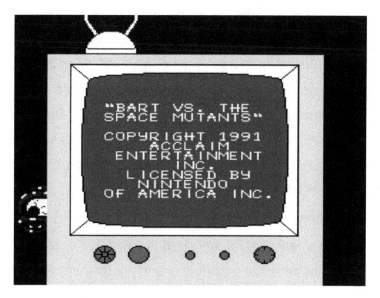

The A-Teams.

Bartmania took hold of America early and inspired much of the merchandise of that era. It seemed that every kid either identified with Bart or just thought he was the character they should slap onto their T-shirts and lunch boxes. And so when it came time to select a protagonist for the first home console game, there was no question that it should be Bart in the spotlight. According to Kitchen:

> We brainstormed a game where each level you were controlling a different character, doing skills appropriate for who they were & Brooks loved it. We went home and Acclaim threw a fit. They were 100% right. It was all about Bart on a skateboard.[7]

His nemeses on the other hand are a head-scratcher. Aliens have invaded Springfield, and apparently the only person who can stop them is a ten year-old kid with X-ray specs. Bart must defeat the aliens by eliminating the items they need to build their ultimate weapons, including purple trinkets, hats, and EXIT signs, while using his X-ray glasses to find and eliminate the alien invaders. This alien invasion premise pulls liberally from the 1988 Roddy Piper vehicle, *They Live*.[8]

The gameplay of *Mutants* is in line with the order of the day, which was side-scrolling action platformers. See Bart run, See Bart jump. He can hop on (some) enemies to take them out, and he can shoot (some) enemies in levels that allow him to use projectiles. His physics are slippery, just like Mario, but he controls like he can't make up his mind. Should Bart run, or should he move faster? It's difficult to do both simultaneously unless the player holds down the jump button while in the air or the all-purpose attack/select button which may accidentally use some of the limited resources available for weapons or the spray paint.

The game's complicated control scheme may be forgiven when considering the item selection menu. Imagineering opted not to include a menu overlay like the one seen in *The Legend of Zelda* or any console RPG ever. Instead, the player must tap the Select button to scroll through the item list (and the pause option), then press that all-purpose B button. Perhaps it's this need to keep the B button available that led to the less sub-par control scheme, but it is a mind-boggling compromise in any side-scrolling platformer released after *Super Mario Bros.* The template was there and Imagineering chose to take a hard left.

All out of bubblegum.

Level design varies wildly from ambitious adventure game to rote platformer. The first level is infamous for its multi-layered approach to the objective of covering up the purple objects that the space mutants are so desperate to find. Bart can walk on a clothesline to knock down towels that cover playground equipment below, use a wrench on a fire hydrant to ruin a freshly painted awning, or even use a coin with the public pay phone to pull a prank call on Moe the bartender so that he'll step outside and Bart can spray his purple apron. The player can also collect coins and purchase a variety of beneficial items in the shops of Downtown Springfield in the first level. This complex array of solutions makes the first level feel like the proof of concept that won the contract for Imagineering. The last level at the Nuclear Power Plant also has some level of thought put into it with its maze of corridors, locked doors, and randomized locations of characters. But then there are the three levels in the middle, all designed to make players pull their hair out with their tiny platforms over dangerous pits and invincible enemies. To the developers' credit, there are checkpoints in the levels that allow players to recover from the game's many unfair deaths but they are few and far between.

The game gives players two chances to take a hit before losing a life, and those hit points remain constant. There are no opportunities for upgrades and no hit point recovery items. It's the kind of anxiety-inducing difficulty curve that some developers adopted to prevent players from finishing a game too quickly. After all, they had to give a kid their forty dollars' worth of video game by dragging it out as long as possible. It harkens back to punishing action-adventures like *Ghosts 'n Goblins* that were falling out of style by the early nineties. There were no quarters to burn here, just the good will of fans of *The Simpsons*.

Purple monkey dishwasher.

The game's art style is... not quite abysmal, but certainly disappointing. One can tell they're looking at the Simpsons, and some of the boss enemies such as Sideshow Bob match their television visages fairly well. But what in Jebus's name happened with Bart? His sprite looks flat, lacking any kind of outline or attempt to match the show's designs. Every game developer understands that the player character—the one piece of art the player must constantly stare at—should be the best-looking art in the game, but not Imagineering and not their *Simpsons* games on NES. Later versions of the game would do a better job both with the characters and environments, but the first and most memorable release on NES just looked like something dragged out of the eighties. Players and fans of *The Simpsons* deserved better by 1991. Speaking of those environments, the first level is the only recognizably *Simpsons* area, with distinctive buildings like Moe's Tavern and the statue of Jebediah Springfield. With the possible exception of the nuclear power plant at the end, every other level is so generic that it could have been designed for any one of Imagineering's many generic platformer games. The museum in level four in particular is just full of enemies that are banal and appropriate for the setting, but not for *The Simpsons*. Again, later ports by other developers would do a better job with their art design.

The game's sound is serviceable with the appropriate beeps and boops that are another example of eighties computer game design on display. The notable aspect of the game's sound is that they managed to squeeze in some character voice samples at a time when that was still an impressive feat on NES. The other noteworthy bit of sound design is that they got the rights to Danny Elfman's theme song from the show. They'll let the player know that they acquired it when they play it at the title screen, during the intro cutscene, in every level, as a short loop in the boss fights, and in every other conceivable place where one might otherwise expect some background music to the action. It certainly feels like they only had budget and/or time for one music track and they're going to flood the player's brain with it.

It was a big license to tackle and Imagineering shot for the stars, unfortunately they missed and ended up somewhere in the swamps of New Jersey.

As vulnerable and beautiful as any of God's creatures.

David Crane, cofounder of Absolute Entertainment, once told a programmer who'd created a port of one of his games, "It looks nice, but take out all that creative stuff." By his estimation, a port—or adaptation as he calls it—should be exactly like the original game without embellishments.[9] The developers of the ports for *Bart vs. the Space Mutants* agreed.

The game may have been a rough prospect when it first launched on NES, but as the first and best known of the early games it received a lot of attention that translated to significant profits. There is no greater evidence of the market's demand for *Simpsons* game merch than the fact that *Bart vs. the Space Mutants* was and remains the *Simpsons* game ported to the greatest number of platforms. From micro computers to consoles and even a LCD handheld version, it's a wonder that the game didn't actually end up on all the platforms, with handheld systems like the Game Boy notably missing from the list.

Let them eat Bart.

But the rest of the gang was all here. North America received ports for IBM PC, Sega Genesis, and Sega Game Gear (with Sega platforms published under Acclaim's Flying Edge label), but that pales in comparison to Europe's showing on additional platforms: ZX Spectrum, Amiga, Commodore 64, Atari ST, Amstrad CPC, Sega Master System, and LCD handheld. International releases were handled by that infamous hoarder of licensed titles, OCEAN Software, and all other ports of the game were developed by Arc Developments in the UK. The notable improvements in later ports of the game would include much improved visuals on Sega Genesis and IBM PC, as well as improved sound and music. Some of these may have crossed the pond but by and large there was a swath of *Bart vs. the Space Mutants* ports that Americans were lucky enough not to see.

A noble wallet embiggens the smallest fan.

Ill-regarded as it was, and tied to a license that began its abysmal home console record right here, *Bart vs. the Space Mutants* remains buried in the past, joining its middling licensed brethren in the first and forgotten category of game history. But Acclaim and Imagineering were just getting started. After all, according to Kitchen, "It sold very very well, and wasn't a bad game, but it could have been superb, given more time."[10] Bolstered by the unquenchable thirst that led to astronomical sales of merchandise featuring *The Simpsons*, the games would keep on comin'.

Notes

1. Dan Ackerman, *The Tetris Effect* (New York: PublicAffairs, 2016).
2. "Indie Gamer Chick Talks To The Amazing Garry Kitchen About Bart vs The Space Mutants" (Twitter, 2020). Archived by James Kinsella on realotakugamer.com. Retrieved 19 March 2021.
3. Al Backiel, "Alex DeMeo interview" (Atari Compendium, 1991). Archived on ataricompendium.com. Retrieved 19 March 2021.
4. "Indie Gamer Chick."
5. Ibid.
6. Ibid.
7. Ibid.
8. Ibid.
9. "PRGE 2017 – David Crane & Garry Kitchen – Portland Retro Gaming Expo 1080p" (YouTube, 2017). Archived by Hans Reutter on youtube.com. Retrieved 19 March 2021.
10. "Indie Gamer Chick."

Chapter 3: The Terrible Outdoors

Bart Simpson's Escape from Camp Deadly - October 1991

The Nintendo Game Boy remained a mystery to me for many years with only a few experiences with the handheld before one was gifted to me in my teens. But I do know that my neighbor Jason had one. He and I became friends after my parents moved us to our longtime Los Angeles suburb in 1989, and while we mostly played outside we did occasionally spend some time with my NES or his Game Boy. And this is how I first played the little platformer called *Bart Simpson's Escape from Camp Deadly*. As with many of these early *Simpsons* game experiences, I found it difficult and obtuse. I remember playing it just once before giving up and asking what other cartridges my neighbor had.

I will not lend you my ears, thanks.

Acclaim was riding high on the success of *Bart vs. the Space Mutants.* Game magazine coverage of the era (and the many, many ports) suggests that the game on NES not only sold extremely well but was a hit at video rental stores as well. It didn't matter that the game itself probably didn't inspire positive word of mouth except by those masochistic players eager for frustratingly challenging gameplay, because 1991 was the year of *The Simpsons.* The characters were slapped onto every conceivable product from mugs[1] to fanny packs[2] and even dining room placemats,[3] and any kid with a game console would have been clamoring to play a game featuring the characters. This bolstered demand and I'm sure left owners of platforms other than the NES wondering when they'd get their *Simpsons* game.

It's certain that the first game's success prompted development of the next wave of games. And where did they start? With that little paragon of handheld gaming: the Nintendo Game Boy. Released in 1989, the Game Boy dominated the handheld game space for the next decade, outperforming its high-powered competitors with low-cost tech that sported a far superior battery life. The handheld famously shipped with a cartridge of *Tetris* that hooked players of all ages and made it ubiquitous as the platform of choice for anyone looking to kill some time in the schoolyard or during commutes. Really, Game Boy was the ur-mobile device. And while the Simpsons had appeared on a few LCD handheld games by 1991, the Game Boy was an altogether different beast.

It may seem strange for Acclaim to veer away from the success on NES to publish on an additional platform, but recall that Imagineering's developers once strived to churn out Atari games in 3–4 months. I'm sure the relatively limited scope of a Game Boy game lent itself to this hyper efficient development ethos and allowed them to split their attention across multiple projects. And this new Game Boy game would be headed up by none other than David Crane, legendary designer of Atari classics like *Pitfall!* and their more recent NES hit *A Boy and His Blob.*

But how would his next game featuring the Simpsons come about? Whatever the timeline, Crane and his team had a *Simpsons* game on Nintendo Game Boy by the end of 1991, just in time for the holiday sales frenzy.

Satanic sacrifice is a seldom utilized game development tool.

The game that became *Bart Simpson's Escape from Camp Deadly* took a bold direction with its design. Namely, it wasn't just a port of the lucrative *Bart vs. the Space Mutants*. It's probably due to the relatively limited hardware packed into the Nintendo Game Boy, but as the game with David Crane's name on it one had to wonder if there was a desire to do something different, and Crane was in a position to make such a decision. In fact, the only *Simpsons* game to see a port on Game Boy was the puzzle-platformer *Krusty's Fun House* (Chapter 6). Every other game was an original creation and it all began with this first game from Imagineering.

The game's premise is as dead-simple as its title implies: Bart and Lisa Simpson have been sent to a summer camp from hell, and they need to get out. The camp is headed by the cruel counselor Ironfist Burns, kicking off Imagineering's strange fascination with relatives of Mr. Burns as the villains. But wait, you might say. Isn't this just the plot of the *Simpsons* episode called "Kamp Krusty"? I mean, the summer camp horror story, the cruel camp activities, bully counselors who are more foe than friend. But that episode of the show didn't premiere until fall of 1992, nearly a year after this game.[4] It's possible that some writer or producer involved in the approval process for *Escape* cribbed the pitch for their episode from this game, but considering that production of one episode of the television show takes about a year, it's more likely a case of serendipitous design. After all, any show worth its salt had a summer camp episode if kids were in the cast.

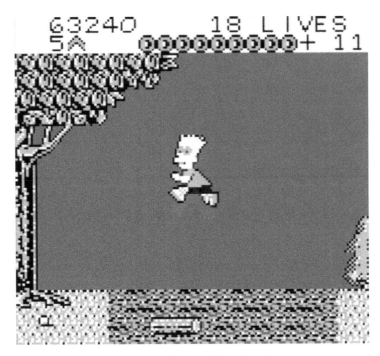

Platforming is good for the glutes.

The law of mascot games in the eighties and early nineties was that it had to be a platformer. It was safe and provided the best opportunity to get a good look at the characters plastered all over the box. And that is one of the most unexpected surprises of this game—the characters look more like their television counterparts than the earlier incarnations on NES. I spent enough time ragging on those mutant designs but it's just such a stark contrast for the sprites on a Game Boy game to look better than NES. I wouldn't call these designs amazing or anything but they look pretty good for a game rendering on a screen 160 pixels wide and 144 pixels tall. Familiar characters like

Bart, Lisa, and Nelson look good for Game Boy, and common enemies like camp counselors and skeletons look appropriately Simpsony. This idealised perspective crumbles a bit when the entire family appears in the finale like a group of strangely familiar mutants, but hey, I'm sure they'd look okay on a tiny Game Boy screen. Some of the adults early on like cafeteria workers and some weirdo named Mad Man Mort also have that Simpson eidonomy, but once again things fall apart when Ironfist Burns himself appears as the final obstacle. It's almost like the artist had to rush out some art at the end and just couldn't get those final characters quite right. But all in all, it's a better-than-expected showing.

Then one sees the environments and it's clear how they were able to dedicate so much memory to good-looking sprites. The environments in *Camp Deadly* are... well, bland. Setting the game in a summer camp never seen on the show gave the artist (that's one artist, folks) free rein to design simple levels with summer camp vibes. Of the game's six levels, three take place in variations of a forest with bits of sewer sprinkled in, two take place in a cafeteria, and one vertically oriented level is on the precarious Mt. Deadly. In short, this game's environments look and feel like they were made with limited time and memory. And, you know, that's fine. If an art compromise must be made I'd rather they lean into character design over environments. Music and sound in the game are... well, the same as *Bart vs. the Space Mutants*, which is to say about as bland as the environments in which they play. It's the same tinny variations and beeps and boops as *Bart vs. the Space Mutants*. The only mildly impressive sound work is that the developers squeezed in Bart's signature line when he dies, and the player will hear it a lot. It's not a *Simpsons* game if Bart doesn't say some garbled version of "Eat my shorts!"

Firing from the hip.

The gameplay is as dead simple as the premise. The player is presented with notably dry objective text at the beginning of each level via either bulletin boards or cutscenes. While *Bart vs. the Space Mutants* made some attempt at fun or humor through the interstitial alien

48

dialogue and prank calls to Moe, *Escape* simply strips that out. I'd excuse it as a limitation of the platform but Imagineering themselves would prove that they can squeeze humorous bits of dialogue into a Game Boy cartridge just a year later in *Bart vs. the Juggernauts* (Chapter 8). But for now we're caught in the mire of this straightforward platformer in which the objectives amount to walk to the right, climb to the top, and walk to the right some more. Anyone who came up playing these games knows the score. Bart's repertoire of abilities while traversing Camp Deadly is surprisingly robust. Rather than simply hop on enemies, Bart is given use of a boomerang to take out foes and spit wads to stun them while waiting for the boomerangs to return. Boomerangs can also be fired at angles dependent on the player's trajectory, with upward attacks if the player throws while jumping up and downward attacks while falling. It takes some getting used to but it makes for more strategic attacks when dealing with vertically variable enemies.

Additional power-ups come in the form of suits that protect Bart from specific enemies. The beekeeper suit allows Bart to walk through bee hives that would otherwise kill him in one hit, the football suit is good for charging through annoying counselor assaults, and there's even a radiation suit for walking through human-sized atoms. Each of these suit gimmicks is utilized only once in a playthrough but they are only obtained after defeating a trio of treehouse toughs with names like Slipshod Sammy and Rebound Rodney. They are kind of hidden and tough to acquire, providing a nice break in the monotony of forest fighting.

And there'll be fights aplenty, because an entire army of counselors and forest creatures lies before the player. The counselors stream in occasionally at first and only along the ground, but they gradually increase in frequency until they're coming out like ninjas on parade. They'll run in from both sides of the screen, jump in at an angle, lob projectiles, and just generally do their best to whittle away the donuts that represent Bart's health until nothing remains. This makes for a game that is pleasantly amusing until it becomes a real slog for survival. Other creatures such as wasps, fish, eagles, and spiders serve to fill out the space between counselor attacks, and I suppose I have to credit the designers for their level design choices. The environments may be monotonous but there's no shortage of obstacles and the difficulty ramp-up is consistent. It's the kind of challenge a kid could spend a few weekends trying to overcome in 1991, and a player familiar with the game can complete it in thirty minutes.

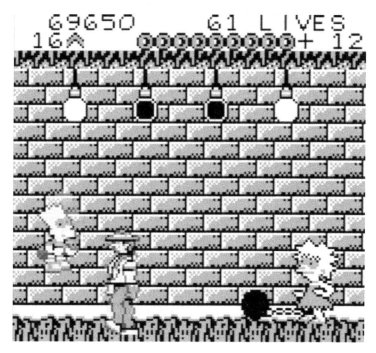

Ugh, more like IronWORST Burns.

The game ultimately feels like a product of an era that has continued to this day on mobile platforms. It's a low-cost, low-energy game designed to capitalize on the popularity of a license that was highly lucrative, and while it improves on the character designs seen in its NES predecessor, the gameplay is a run-of-the-mill platformer slog and lacks any of the charm of the TV show. It's good business at the expense of, you know, a positive reputation and fun for players. Future *Simpsons* games on Game Boy will have their ups and downs (mostly down), but they'll at least try to break away from the formula to try something new.

51

Notes

1. "Marge Simpson Thank You It's My Specialty The Simpsons Mug" (Mug Barista, 2020). Retrieved 19 March 2021.

2. Zach Nagle and Madeline Berger, "Our Favorite Vintage Fanny Packs" (Ragstock, 2018). Retrieved 19 March 2021.

3. "1990s Vintage The Simpsons Placemats / Placemat Set" (Depop, 2020). Retrieved 19 March 2021.

4. "Kamp Krusty," *The Simpsons* (Fox Television, 1992). Directed by Mark Kirkland and written by David M. Stern.

Chapter 4: The Travelogue

Bart vs. the World – November 1991

I was in college when I discovered the existence of *Bart vs. the World*, or the fact that there were more than, like, five *Simpsons* games altogether. I'd been writing game walkthroughs for a bit and decided these poor, neglected *Simpsons* games needed some kind of coverage, and *Bart vs. the World* was among the first that I selected. My expectations were low, but that was just the way to experience the best *Simpsons* game on the NES.

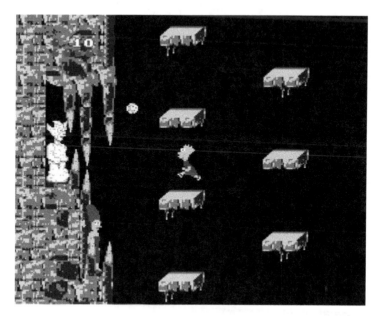

The age of discovery.

While development of *Escape from Camp Deadly* on Game Boy moved along in the middle of 1991, Acclaim knew they couldn't rest on their NES laurels. A direct follow-up to *Bart vs. the Space Mutants* had to ship by December so they could rake in those sweet holiday moneys, and Imagineering was back to bite off a piece of that pie as well. It's clear that Imagineering had to bolster their staff numbers in order to cover concurrent development between the Game Boy and NES games. David Crane split off to lead development of the Game Boy title, while Dan Kitchen—one of the cofounders of the company—led the NES sequel along with programmer Roger Booth and designer Barry Marx, all of whom worked on the previous NES *Simpsons* game.

The game shipped just seven months after *Bart vs. the Space Mutants*, and considering how quickly Acclaim followed up with a NES sequel, it's surprising to learn that Acclaim didn't start on it right away. Lead designer Dan Kitchen explains, "[After] we finished *Bart vs. The Space Mutants*, Acclaim came to us about 6 months later to discuss a sequel."[1] According to Dan, they were inspired by the fact that the show continued its meteoric rise in popularity. The third season premiered in fall of 1991 and is by all accounts the beginning of the golden era of the television show. No one could stop the show's pop culture dominance and the new game had to reflect that attitude. They decided that space mutants weren't enough—this time, Bart would take on the world. Garry Kitchen, another cofounder at Imagineering, recalls the initial inspiration for the sequel: "All I wanted from *Bart vs. the World* was Bart skateboarding down the Great Wall of China. I swear, that was the entire reason for pitching the idea."[2] Fortunately, the team was given more time to realize this new direction for the sequel, with Dan estimating they had roughly six months to design and build the game.[3]

Two cars in every garage and a Simpson on every TV.

Bart vs. the World does as the title suggests and pits the player as Bart against the world, or more precisely obstacles and enemies from four locations around the world. Through a contrived but amusing series of events, Bart is selected to go on a global treasure hunt that leads him to China, the North Pole, Egypt, and Hollywood. The contest turns out to be a ruse perpetrated by the self-avowed nemesis of the Simpsons, Mr. Burns. Each location features two or three platform levels and an additional assortment of parlor and puzzle mini games that reward the player with additional treasures and lives. These mini games were regarded as odd additions at the time, but they provided an interesting array of amusements as a break between the more challenging platforming segments.

Some of the mini games harken back to video game classics such as the card match mini game from *Super Mario Bros. 3* and *Root Beer Tapper*. Tile sliding puzzles are another childhood classic in which the player shuffles a set of tiles around on a grid in order to complete an image of one of the game's characters. Oddly enough, the trivia game is the least interesting to me, but that may only be because *Simpsons* trivia is more fun with other people at a bar. Other games such as a three shell game and a slot machine are there for the kids who couldn't wait to get to Vegas. The mini games are optional while the platform levels must be completed to proceed to the final boss of each of the four locations. The boss characters, who all hail from distant branches of the Burns family tree, are rudimentary battles that are nonetheless far more fun to fight than those of the previous game. Dan recalls working with designer Barry Marx on those boss designs: "Acclaim wanted the concept of bosses. Barry and I thought it would fit in well with the overall story if there [sic] turned out to all be relatives of Mr. Burns."[4]

The first and most notable difference in gameplay between the last game and this one is that the pretense of adventure game design is completely dropped. There are no more ancillary items to collect, no inventory menus to navigate. The treasures collected throughout levels are simply for points and bonuses at the end of the game (more on that later). Dan remembers how this change in design from the first game came about:

> Initially, Fox wanted the game to highlight Krusty the clown. Thus all the cheap Krusty merch scattered about. Acclaim wanted the game to be more of a Mario-style 'get to the end of the level' game. So we didn't focus on the puzzle solving aspect.[5]

While this makes the progression of each platform level a much more straightforward affair compared to the complexity of the source television material, the expanded focus on platform level design makes those portions of the game surprisingly fun.

Vertical scrolling allows for expanded exploration of the space and is in fact an essential aspect of the game's goal of hunting for treasures. While the slippery *Super Mario*-style physics from the first game return here, jumping onto platforms is no longer a form of cruel and unusual punishment. They're a bit wider, but still challenging. Of course, some players still found the platform traversal too difficult. Dan regrets some of the level design choices: "Back then players wanted the games to be harder. I personally look back on [many] games I worked on and wish I had [tweaked] them to be easier. I never liked thin platforms and jumps to nowhere."[6] The diametric difference in level design is welcome and while the disconnect from the show is palpable, I appreciate the effort to streamline the gameplay. It's just... actually fun to play the game. It's fun enough that I'd recommend *Bart vs. the World* to anyone seeking out new NES games to discover. The rough reputation of the 8-bit *Simpsons* games causes *World* to unfairly slip between the cracks. That said, the one gameplay aspect that disappoints me is the return of the same wonky controls in which the player can't simply hold B to run and A to jump, again like any game after *Super Mario Bros.* should have utilized. Ostensibly, this was done to allow the player the use of the B button for Bart's projectile weapons, but it feels bad just the same.

Do the Bartman all over ancient history.

The game also introduces a wider set of abilities for Bart. In addition to projectiles such as firecrackers to throw at enemies, players can now seek out Bartman icons to gain temporary flying ability, as well as the ability to climb on certain parts of the environment such as ship masts and Sphinx legs. This adds an element of variety to traversal that was sorely missing from *Mutants* and makes exploration of the platformer levels more interesting. It turns out that the inclusion of Bartman (both in this game and the next one, see Chapter 9) was actually at the behest of Fox and/or Gracie Films.[7]

While level design showed a marked improvement, the game's art remained similarly banal, as it would for all of

Imagineering's *Simpsons* games. They repurposed the same Bart and Simpson character sprites from the first game, only adding a modified version of the same Bart sprite for the Bartman transformations. While the enemy variety was far better than the previous game's penchant for little creatures that hop up and down, the designs remained vaguely connected to the world of *The Simpsons*. Take the first level on a Chinese junk, which is a type of ancient ship. The enemies encountered here are primarily Chinese sailors circa the nineteenth century, evident by their tonsured hair and black cotton outfits typical of laborers during the period. Besides the weirdly casual racism (common of many cartoons of the era), the designs are simple and uninspired. However, according to Dan, it was done with some measure of review and approval: "We worked very closely with [Matt Groening's] team to make sure all the characters, humans and non-humans, were all created in that Simpson's [sic] style. Once we created a few characters that they approved, it was easier to get the look right."[8]

One can argue that there was only so much programmers could squeeze onto the NES, but that argument don't fly by 1992. This applies to all human enemies encountered in the game, as well as other creatures such as dragons or skeletons. As with *Mutants*, it's all generic enough that it could be in some other game and there'd be no difference. Art design in levels is similarly bland but for a few instances such as in Egypt where a Sphinx head is shaped to look like Krusty the clown. Some of the environments look good in spite of their irrelevance to *The Simpsons*, such as those in the aforementioned Egypt area and the Hollywood levels after it. There the levels demonstrate rich backgrounds and themed enemies to match, and the variety helps prevent any sense of monotony. The level design wasn't exactly unified but it was still a lot more fun than what we got in *Mutants*. Dan remembers the design of one of the game's best areas: "I recall I wanted to put Bart somehow on a Pirate Ship. That was a joke around Acclaim's dev department. The question was how to place Bart back in the days of the pirates. That's when the Hollywood level was thought of."[9] The soundscape was unfortunately as lacking as the previous entry on NES, and while the music (composed by Mark Van Hecke once again) is no longer just the *Simpsons* theme on loop, it's also nothing to write home about.

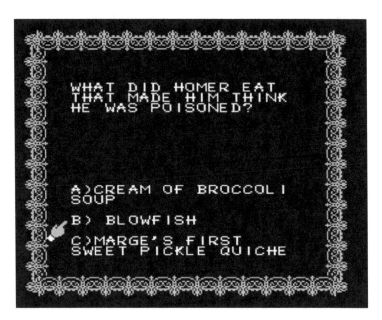

WHAT DID HOMER EAT
THAT MADE HIM THINK
HE WAS POISONED?

A)CREAM OF BROCCOLI
SOUP

B) BLOWFISH

C)MARGE'S FIRST
SWEET PICKLE QUICHE

Didn't even break a sweat.

This roller coaster of a chapter may make it seem like the game's not worth playing, but as I mentioned above it is an absolute gem in the *Simpsons* game catalog. One design choice that ultimately swayed me was the game's implementation of the unique Krusty treasures in each platform level. They are usually hidden and require thorough exploration to discover them all. And while they do have a practical benefit—granting 2000 bonus points that go toward earning extra lives—they are also required for unlocking the secret final level in the Hollywood area. The designers took a page from the notoriously cruel *Ghouls 'n Ghosts* by including two endings: one good, one bad. The bad ending plays out if the player completes all the other levels and misses any of the unique Krusty treasures, leading to a frustrating "princess in another castle" scenario. This alone may make *Bart vs. the World* seem especially cruel, but that good ending absolutely makes up for the added completion requirements. I'll go so far as to say the good ending is one of the best *Simpsons* game endings ever, and I've seen them all. The reward for making it to the end isn't just a series of text boxes or images but a full-on interactive sequence in which the player controls Bart as he throws pies at Mr. Burns and Smithers. It's as juvenile and simple as it sounds, but man, it feels *so good* to be able to wallop the characters with pies in the face after the trials and tribulations leading up to it. I don't know, maybe it just felt good to see the rich old jerk get his comeuppance. If you can't eat the rich, make the rich eat pie.

And now you know: I love *Bart vs. the World*! It's a complicated affair with plenty to dislike, but I still happily return to the game decades after it silently released in the wake of Bartmania. It may not have had the lasting impact of the comparatively dismal *Bart vs. the Space Mutants* but it is certainly the diamond in the rough of these *Simpsons* NES games.

The dreaded conehead attack.

The video game industry may have solidified into a network of platforms that can all play more or less the same games, but the early nineties was still a wild west of hardware companies and platforms. *Bart vs. the Space Mutants* released into that environment on more than a dozen platforms. However, things had begun to change. The micro computers that dominated the American and especially European landscapes were coalescing into a relatively small list of platforms while Nintendo's and Sega's 16-bit consoles swooped into market dominance. The ports that were made for *Bart vs. the World* reflected the changing times. Besides the NES, the game made it onto only four platforms: Sega's Master System and handheld Game Gear from Acclaim, and the Atari ST and Amiga from Virgin Interactive in Europe. As with *Mutants*, *World* received significant visual upgrades in the hands of Arc Developments, the same company that ported *Bart vs. the Space Mutants*. While some versions of *Mutants* were severely compromised to fit them onto older computers, the Amiga and Atari ST were relative powerhouses and the *World* ports had no such compromises. Regardless of platform, gameplay remained the same.

I'll tell you where you can put your freakin' sody, too!

Bart vs. the World was superior to its predecessor in many ways, but it arrived at a time when so-so platformers on the NES were on their way out. And while Acclaim would soon make the jump to 16-bit consoles, they still had one more Bart game to spring onto 8-bit fans.

Notes

1. "Indie Gamer Chick Talks To Dan Kitchen About Bart vs The World/Bartman Meets Radioactive Man" (Twitter, 2020). Archived by James Kinsella on realotakugamer.com. Retrieved 19 March 2021.

2. "Indie Gamer Chick Talks To The Amazing Garry Kitchen About Bart vs The Space Mutants" (Twitter, 2020). Archived by James Kinsella on realotakugamer.com. Retrieved 19 March 2021.

3. "Indie Gamer Chick Talks To Dan Kitchen."

4. Ibid.

5. Ibid.

6. Ibid.

7. Ibid.

8. Ibid.

9. Ibid.

Chapter 5: The Weirdness Abounds

Bart's House of Weirdness - January 1992

There are few games whose existence has surprised me. There's *James Pond: RoboCod*, a platformer game about a fish spy with a robot suit that seemed too fun to have flown under everyone's radar. The *King of the Hill* PC game (as in the Fox Television sitcom) was a doozy. And of the *Simpsons* games, it is the appropriately titled *Bart's House of Weirdness* that shocked me. Here was a game published by Japanese publisher Konami, only released on the IBM PC platform, and so richly drawn and animated that I couldn't believe it just released and disappeared like so much abandonware. It was the first retro *Simpsons* game I actively sought to find on eBay and it's been in my collection for nearly two decades. It's a shame it wasn't better than it turned out.

Spending the big bucks.

Acclaim was raking in the dough from its *Simpsons* game releases throughout 1991, but the company's games were conspicuously absent from home computer platforms. That would be because Konami—which had its own *Simpsons* hit on its hands from the early 1991 release of *The Simpsons* arcade game—was the only game in PC town. Konami's *Simpsons* game publishing was a brief run: *The Simpsons Arcade* for IBM PC and Commodore 64, and *Bart's House of Weirdness* exclusively on IBM PC. The former were conversions of that eponymous arcade game that were fairly impressive just for re-creating the experience on home platforms (although not exactly eye-popping in the case of the Commodore 64 port), and all three games were released to the North American PC market in early 1992. There's no record to support my belief that Konami did hold exclusive rights to publish *Simpsons* games on PC, but Konami's brief monopoly can only be explained by an early deal with Fox to make *Simpsons* games on the platforms that Acclaim hadn't already scooped up.

Development duties were contracted out to Distinctive Software Inc., or DSI, which was established by teenage entrepreneurs Jeff Sember and Don Mattrick in Vancouver, British Columbia in 1982. The company spent the eighties growing into a game publisher and developer employing more than seventy people to work on projects for various clients, including a whole boatload of games for Konami. In 1991 alone—the year of development for *Bart's House of Weirdness*—you'll find *Mission: Impossible*, *Bill Elliott's NASCAR Challenge*, and *Teenage Mutant Ninja Turtles: Manhattan Missions*. The team for *Bart's House of Weirdness* was relatively small, but comparable to the team sizes on other *Simpsons* games of the era with about a dozen people assigned to the project.

DSI's work on *Bart's House of Weirdness* looks to have wrapped by the end of 1991, which would be their one shot with a *Simpsons* game before being acquired by Electronic Arts that same year to become EA Canada, maker of sports games and home to the biggest game test center in North America. Matrick and the other studio heads would get their payout and go on to become big cheeses at EA and other companies in the game industry.

Easy for you to say.

I'm going to start with the obvious: the game looks amazing, both for a *Simpsons* game and a PC game of this vintage. Although not developed internally at Konami, the game exhibits the same level of quality and care that Konami poured into their *Simpsons Arcade* project. That is a credit to DSI's craftsmanship and a stark contrast to the work coming out of the *Simpsons* games developed for consoles. I won't judge the console developers too harshly—few NES games could hope to compete with PC games on a graphical level. The hardware on a typical IBM PC in 1992 was just inherently more powerful than the

NES's dated processors. Still, *Bart's House of Weirdness*, as well as the PC version of *The Simpsons Arcade* that launched alongside it, set a graphical standard for *Simpsons* games that wouldn't be matched until the 16-bit games.

I was curious about the source of the art on display, and one name stands out in the credits: Athena Bax, who was credited as a co-designer and sole artist on the game. She remains an active member of the arts community in her native Vancouver and notes in her bio that her career began at DSI in 1987.[1] This is a big deal as I research early *Simpsons* games because there are virtually no women credited at these development companies of the eighties and early nineties (a problem that persists to this day). It's also significant that Bax is the sole artist on what is undoubtedly the best-looking of the first wave of *Simpsons* games. Improved hardware may have enabled the high level of art polish but skill is skill.

And that skill is on display from the get go. *Bart's House of Weirdness* begins with its own take on the heavenly cloud reveal from the television show and includes a few scenes lifted straight from the source. It may appear crude now but this was the best video game version of the introduction on a home platform to that point and for some time afterward. The game offers versions of the program for Tandy, EGA, and MCGA graphical displays, and while MCGA is the best option for anyone on a modern computer, the other versions still look impressive for their time. Gameplay art is just as good-looking as the intro cutscene with big sprites that actually look like the characters and enemy sprites that are big and expressive, providing a bestiary that's fun to look at as they pummel the player. It's also clear that the artist paid special attention to the environments. The scenes are all packed with enough detail and visual gags that make it clear the creators understood and cared about the source material. If I have any criticism, it's that environments look too perfect, like drawings made with a ruler firmly in hand for each and every line. Some scenes just lacked a certain *Simpsons* wonkiness, the curves and imperfections that characterized a *Simpsons* episode of the early seasons. Some people may have found the wild inconsistency of the art direction on the television show to be grating but I've always enjoyed it, and this game could've done with a little of the same wonky magic.

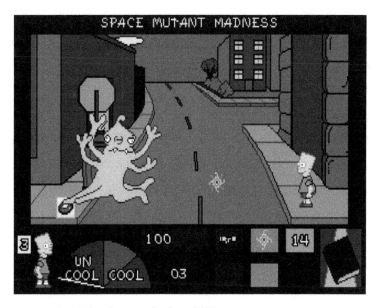

Look both ways before killing space mutants.

The game's user interface, on the other hand, is designed to be all wonk, with garish colors and wobbly fonts right out of a nineties Lisa Frank catalog. The game's HUD covers all the key information such as health and weapon caches in an interesting way that beats the heck out of the white text on black that always felt like an afterthought in other games. The overall area for displaying the actual characters and environments is reduced as a result and I have no doubt that this was a decision made in the wake of the adventure game boom and as a practical measure to reduce the amount of art they needed to generate for each screen.

Another aspect of the game I love is the sound design, and specifically the music. The game has an actual soundtrack! In a *Simpsons* game! They're not all bangers but the sound desert of past (and future) *Simpsons* home releases sits in stark contrast to the breadth of music available in *Bart's House of Weirdness*. The designers were so proud of their soundtrack that they provided a cassette tape player in Bart's room just for the player to check out each of the tracks. Composers J. Daniel Scott, Traz Damji, Michael J. Sokyrka, Brian Plank, Krisjan Hatlelid, and Tara deserve the praise. Sound effects during gameplay were not as impressive but accomplished their task, and perhaps most notable is the inclusion of some pretty high quality samples of Nancy Cartwright's voice as Bart. Compact discs were still a few years away as the medium that unlocked disk space for voices galore, so it's impressive that DSI squeezed even this modest voice acting onto the 1.2 MB of drive space available on the 5 1/4 inch floppy disks.

Bart's dream, your nightmare.

The game's six levels and myriad hub areas are all structured as a series of distractions to pass the time after Bart is grounded to his room. It's a simple opportunity for Bartesque hi-jinks and feels like a premise pulled from the animated interstitial shorts on the *Tracey Ullman Show,* or the first season of the sitcom at the latest. Enemy characters like the Babysitter Bandit and Sideshow Bob are pulled right out of that first season of the show, although there are hints of characters and jokes from the second season as well. The developers clearly understood the source material and threw in all kinds of visual nods and gags, but there is a notable absence: dialogue. I've previously called out the serviceable but dry dialogue in past games, though I still appreciate their attempts. *Bart's House of Weirdness* skips it altogether, choosing instead to convey simple instructions and otherwise move the plot forward with silent slideshows of scenes traced in from animation cells. The bulk of the plot is instead written into the manual for players who needed an extra bit of incentive on their journey through Bart's ten-year old psyche.

I've been avoiding this topic but it looms over everything, and ultimately decides this game's place in the pantheon of *Simpsons* titles: gameplay design. *Bart's House of Weirdness* looks like a typical side-scrolling action game but the designers made certain choices that make the game as difficult as all get out and creates an experience quite different from the *Simpsons* games released to that point.

Let's start with a real doozy: the controls. Players have the option to plug in a joystick or use the keyboard to guide Bart through each of the areas in the game. Joystick is a good option to try out but I found the keyboard more amenable to my methodical approach. And methodical is good when faced with a side-scrolling action game in which the player character is locked into canned animations with no physics involved at all. This style of movement was popularized in cinematic platformers such as *The Prince of Persia* and *Another World*, but the transposition to *Bart's House of Weirdness* just didn't fit with the fast-paced combat. The player has the option to jump straight up, jump forward a short distance, and jump forward across half the screen. And... that's it. This might work well in those games with more open and exploratory environments, but a game in which each screen absolutely bombards the player with hazards should require more finesse in its movements.

Another aspect of player movement that really grates is Bart's knockback animation when his sprite is hit by enemies. Bart is flung back in a huge arc that the player has no control over, forced to sit back and watch as Bart glides into a pit or sewer acid. The game constrains movement so much that it almost feels like a tactical game. Each screen is an assessment of the hazards and the optimal path forward, that is when the cruel design allows even a moment to take in the scene before being forced to react. I complained about controls in Bart's NES outings as well, but they were at least more intuitive with the ability to hold buttons to gain height and distance, providing more dynamic gameplay. *Bart's House of Weirdness* is content to leverage the PC's legacy of save scumming as a means to deal with the difficulty, and perhaps this design methodology is justified when dealing with a game that can be completed by experienced players in twenty minutes.

Bart said f*ck tha police.

The game's screen-by-screen design is rooted in a fundamental limitation of PC games that had to run on older hardware: side-scrolling. PC games were notoriously incapable of accomplishing a feat that consoles mastered by the late eighties. Even Nintendo, masters of the side-scroller, were unable to release a port of *Super Mario Bros.* on PC that included scrolling levels. This forced the game designers to approach *Bart's House of Weirdness* as many designers of PC games did, with individual screens each jam-packed with enough hazards and enemies to justify the price. Nonetheless, the level design felt quaint by 1992. Players who did traverse the wilds of Bart's imagination were greeted with few secrets but enough that there was encouragement to try again after each inevitable and swift death. They even fell back on that old standby of scores and leaderboards. Perhaps they simply foresaw the future of speedrunning... but it feels more like the designers' minds were firmly rooted in the past.

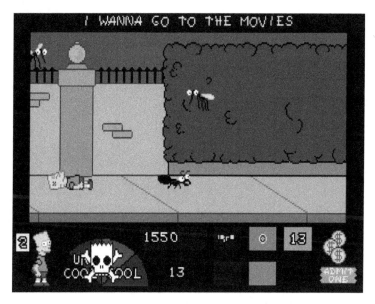

I, for one, welcome our new insect overlords.

The adventure culminates in Krustyland with a feeble fight against Sideshow Bob. The fight requires a precise number of hits with Bart's big burp gun because there are precisely thirteen burp bullets in the entire level, no more, no less. If the player fails to find all the ammo or simply misses a shot, it's time to start the level over again. This final act of malicious design sums up what the game is all about. It's an exercise in memorization of enemy patterns and repetition, repetition, repetition. It looks and sounds amazing and it's the kind of game that any kid who owned a PC would have loved to boot up as a means to fill out the summer days, but now it just feels like a masochistic journey down the Springfield gutter.

Notes

1. Athena Bax, "BIOGRAPHY / ABOUT" (2018). Archived by Internet Archive on web.archive.org. Retrieved 19 March 2021.

Chapter 6: The Rodents of His Discontent

Krusty's Fun House – June 1992

Krusty's Fun House is one of those games that was always just... there. You'd see it in magazines, on store shelves, in game bins, at your friend's house, and sometimes it mysteriously turned up in your game collection. Name a game platform of the early nineties and there it was. It wanted to be owned and played by everyone, existing in all places and realities. *Krusty's Fun House* wanted to conquer the world.

Krusty's Fun House just wanted to be loved.

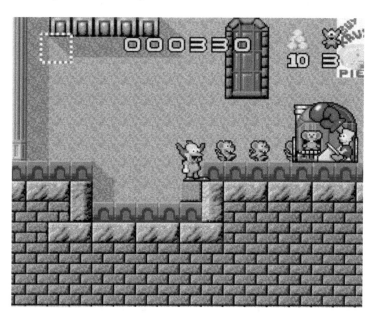

It's alright, I hear rats like to be squished.

Krusty's Fun House (or *Krusty's Super Fun House* on some platforms) was a strange amalgam of opportunistic game production and intellectual property. The game's origins are rooted in the Amiga computer development scene of the United Kingdom, where two designers named Patrick Fox and Scott Williams formed a development company appropriately named Fox Williams. The designer-developers signed with a sports game developer called Audiogenic to release their first game on Amiga platforms: *Rat Trap*. The game combines traditional side-scrolling and platform jumping with the rat herding and block placement mechanics that allow the player to complete a simple objective: kill 'em all. That wasn't the marketing slogan but it's the goal for every one of the game's fifty-plus levels. The premise was undoubtedly informed by the wild success of *Lemmings* by DMA Design, which also started out on the Amiga platform.

The game would have gone on to release on additional platforms, except our old friend Acclaim swooped in to purchase the rights to the game with the intent to turn it into a different series altogether. They worked with Audiogenic and Fox Williams to turn the cutesy mouse genocide game into the cutesy mouse genocide game featuring Krusty the clown. The main character, mice, and enemies all received graphical updates to fit them into the *Simpsons* universe, with additional minor visual tweaks and new screens for the introduction and finale, but environments remained largely similar to *Rat Trap.*

Audiogenic would go on to be purchased by Codemasters for their sports game development talent, but not before teaming up with Fox Williams for one more round of platformer madness. The final game from the Fox Williams collaboration is *Bubble and Squeak* from 1993, published on the Sega Mega Drive by Sunsoft and then the Amiga by Audiogenic. Like *Krusty's Fun House*, *Bubble and Squeak* features a protagonist (Bubble) manipulating an AI-controlled character (Squeak) to navigate side-scroller platform levels. It's easy to see the connection between the two. Patrick Fox and Scott Williams would continue to work in the video game industry for some time, but never again as Fox Williams.

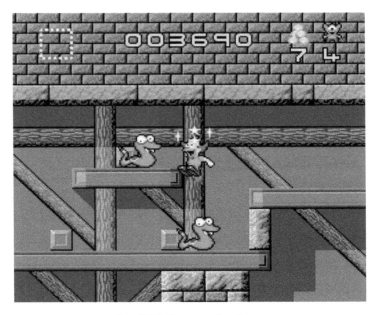

Why did it have to be derps...

It must have been an easy choice for Acclaim to look at their stable of licenses and decide that Krusty would be a good protagonist for the newly christened *Krusty's Fun House*. *The Simpsons* was still a hugely popular show in 1992, but Bart's place as the breakout star had begun to fade almost as quickly as he had arrived. That wouldn't dissuade Acclaim from releasing more games starring Bart, but they probably realized they had to diversify. The problem was solved when this funny puzzle game called *Rat Trap* came knocking at their door.

The game's premise is fitting for a character renowned for his greed and penchant for slapping his name on any product, which in itself is commentary on Fox's eager shilling of the *Simpsons* license. In this instance, Krusty owns a fun house that has become overrun with mischievous rats. In an uncharacteristic turn, Krusty decides to handle the problem himself and herd the rats into traps placed in each of the game's maze-like levels. Bart and Homer assist on trap duty, as well as Krusty's sidekicks Corporal Punishment and Sideshow Mel. This simply means that the trap machine animations from *Rat Trap* now include one of the aforementioned character sprites as well. This is, after all, a *Simpsons* game. And that about covers the objectives. The complexity and difficulty of the solutions increases over time, but the objective is never more complicated than guiding the rats through the levels.

The manner in which the player guides the rats is the puzzle side of this platformer. The key mechanic for the player is the ability to pick up and drop one of several types of blocks that appear in the levels. Most blocks can be used to build steps for the rats to reach other areas and as platforms for the player. Pipe blocks are introduced early on and come in straight and curved configurations, used to complete long pipes which push rats along from one end to the other. There are blowers... glass jars... springs... all blocks with the same dimensions and their own properties. All levels are constructed with these objects as the, erm, building blocks.

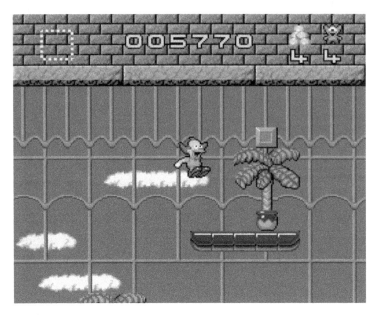

The occasional glimpse of a world beyond blocks.

While there is some freedom in the player's approach to the puzzles in each level, most are designed with a specific solution in mind. Block and rat placement is identical each time the level is loaded. Furthermore, because the rats are autonomous and will just start walking in a given direction, the player doesn't always have the time to leisurely explore the level to plan out a route to the trap machine. One early example is a level in which the rats begin walking as usual while the player freely explores the level's labyrinth of tunnels and blocks. What doesn't become clear until it's too late is that the rats can eventually fall into a pit from which there is no escape, which might sound ideal when trapping rats but not for a level in which every last rat must be deposited into the death machine. So the level becomes unwinnable and the player is forced to forfeit to return to the world hub, losing a life in the process. This harsh lesson instills a certain anxiety for the player that forces thorough and rapid exploration to ensure the rats don't end up where they shouldn't be.

It's a strange way to ramp up the pressure in a game that already includes other, more immediate hazards. Enemies such as snakes, aliens, flying pigs, and giant birds patrol the levels to harm Krusty, who becomes visibly tired when he's low on health. These guardians of the rats aren't too smart or difficult to take out, but the damage they deal over time can certainly lead to the loss of another precious life. Dropping too far a distance (about two screen heights) can also cause damage or just straight-up kill Krusty. There are health items to replenish health of course, and points and Krusty dolls that can be accrued to retain as many extra lives as possible. Then there are the pies and super balls, which can both be used to fend off attackers. Super balls are also used to destroy the crumbling blocks that are sometimes in the way and are handy for their ability to bounce off walls for sweet ricochet shots.

You did the thing! Now remember this because you don't get to save.

All of this makes for a chaotic puzzle game that certainly has more in common with *Super Mario Bros.* than *Tetris.* The art design is similarly chaotic with all kinds of colors and patterns scattered around the environments. Knowing that the game is merely a reskin of a preexisting game, it's clear that the fun house concept was derived from the mélange of styles that Fox Williams and Audiogenic had already created. But there's a method to the madness. The game is divided into five hub sections that each consists of anywhere from eight to fourteen levels per section, and each section's levels have a unique visual style. For example, the first section is a sort of warehouse motif, while the second section has pipes running everywhere. My personal favorite environment is the outdoor levels of the final section where green trees and a night sky are the dominant landscape. It lends the game a melancholy mood that fits the conclusion of a game about killing hundreds of rats. The character designs from Krusty to all the goofy enemies don't particularly fit with the environment design, but they do have the trademark *Simpsons* look to them and are a step above the character art of games released prior to this point. It's a strange triumph but one that is critically important when translating a property as widely known as *The Simpsons* to a video game.

Rounding out the requisite discussion categories is sound and music, which aren't exactly shining examples of their respective disciplines but did accomplish their objectives. Sound effects are simple but scattered effectively to fill the large spaces with some sense of place. Surprisingly, the game includes numerous voice clips of Dan Castellaneta as Krusty the clown, which goes a long way to connect the game to its source material. Of course there is no ambient sound in any of the cavernous levels, making the whole affair perhaps creepier than the designers intended.

There to balance out the creepy silence is the game's soundtrack, which consists of a variety of jaunty tunes that lend the game a carnival feel, fitting for a fun house. Music was composed by a variety of groups for the different versions of the game and while there is some variety in the tracks, it's not enough variety for all those levels. Originally, however, Acclaim producer Paul Provenzao recalls that Matt Groening wanted a more rich musical landscape for the weird little puzzle game. As he shared in an interview on the *Talking Simpsons* podcast, "I still have this thing, this cassette that he sent over with suggestions for music for the game. And it was like Nino Rota music, and all this really intense, kind of orchestral stuff."[1] That would have made an already weird game absolutely resplendent, but alas, Matt Groening's whims were denied.

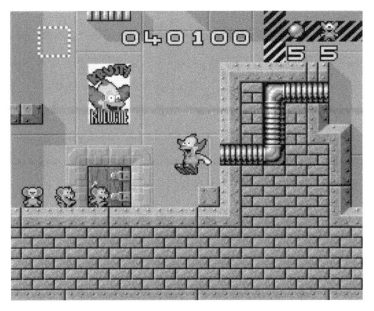

Flying high on Krusty Kologne.

There's the concept in game development of the lead platform, sometimes referred to as the lead SKU (an old merchandising acronym for "stock keeping unit"). This means developing the best version of the game on a specific platform and then iterating out versions of the game for other platforms. Sometimes this means developing on the latest and greatest hardware and then developing versions of the game with reduced graphics or gameplay to run on other systems. Other times, it means creating a game for the lowest common denominator at the risk of game complexity or graphic performance.

It's tough to say for certain which version of *Krusty's Fun House* was that lead version, but I'd guess that Audiogenic's focus on the Amiga means they started there and then branched out into the game's seven other ports. All in all, the game was released on NES, Nintendo Game Boy, Super NES, Sega Genesis, Sega Master System, Sega Game Gear, IBM PC, and of course Amiga computers. Each version has the same number of levels and the same elements, but the game naturally looked and played better on some platforms. In addition to Amiga, the best-looking and most playable versions of the game were for SNES, Sega Genesis, and PC. While the games on other platforms still contained the same gameplay, they were hindered by reduced graphics (such as Bart and Homer being completely missing on NES), reduced screen sizes for handheld platforms, and music that sounded noticeably tinny compared to the improved sound capabilities from other platforms. The core game was always there and players across the spectrum of platforms could get their rat-smashin' fix as they pleased.

Some of these ports are not like the others.

Krusty's Fun House stands out not for its gameplay but for its audacity to exist. It featured a bit player from an animated sitcom whose stars were too busy to spend too much time in a strange little puzzle-platformer. And when opportunity knocked, the developers decided they'd send in the clown.

Notes

1. Bob Mackey, Henry Gilbert, and Chris Antista, "Talking Simpsons Interviews Paul Provenzano," *Talking Simpsons* (Patreon, 2017). Retrieved 2 April 2018.

Chapter 7: The Lynchian Landscape

Bart's Nightmare - September 1992

Video stores proliferated in the eighties as the VHS cassette tape became the dominant medium for viewing movies and television episodes away from the confines of movie theaters, cable, and the public airwaves. The other medium to blow up in the eighties was the video game in the form of cartridges. These sturdy entertainment delivery systems made them ideal for lending out to game-hungry kids with small budgets or a need for constant games in the rotation. Companies like Nintendo fought this of course. They argued it stole revenue out of their pockets if customers could merely rent and complete games for just a few dollars. And while the law in Japan agreed and killed the video game rental market, America would have none of that. The bastion of capitalism would let the free market decide the fates of game companies and video stores.

Kids in the eighties and nineties benefited from these vast networks of game rental locations, as well as the wonders of hindsight. We could now rent games and find out whether they were worth our time and small amounts of money, abandoning the costly guessing game of picking up games at full price. And the more games we played, the more experience we had in selective playing.

Some company names would become synonymous with high-quality, fun experiences. Other companies carried the distinct aroma of frustration and boredom. Licenses helped to offset such associations like a spritz of perfume over a sweaty armpit, but even eau du license could carry the scent of failure.

The Simpsons had six games bearing their name published by fall of 1992, and while the television show was reaching its fullest potential as an animated comedy powerhouse, the games were still struggling to reach similar heights. Some of that limitation was technology—it was simply impossible to match the visual grandeur of the show on the consoles and PCs of the time. And the other and perhaps far more important factor was game design. Acclaim was just not swinging for the fences with their attempts to publish games that were developed within their budgets. They were looking for developers who could create games that were good enough to sell and earn a profit. Maybe it's tough to design a good game around a show that doesn't lend itself to the action-platformers that dominated that era. But they tried, God bless 'em, and some kids played them, but not this kid. I'd seen enough to not necessarily dislike the *Simpsons* games, but certainly to pass over them in favor of something more interesting. This is how I missed nearly all the *Simpsons* games during my formative 16-bit years, including the appropriately titled *Bart's Nightmare*. Why risk renting this when I could grab a *Super Star Wars* or *World of Illusion?* I was just a risk-averse kid with a penchant for the safe bet.

Nothing's safe on these twisted streets.

Outside of a brief flirtation with Audiogenic to develop a strange puzzle game starring Krusty the clown, Acclaim had been pretty faithful to Imagineering. Every *Simpsons* game from the company to date had been developed by the New Jersey-based developer. Now as I've previously written, those games weren't always a hit. It's tough to say if Acclaim's next move was influenced by quality or cost, but for one reason or another, Acclaim turned away from their partners at Imagineering and shopped around for a new developer to work on their 16-bit *Simpsons* games. According to Garry Kitchen, cofounder at Imagineering, it was all part of an executive shuffle:

> Acclaim was happy, they made lots of $$ and kept hiring us for *Simpsons* games. By the time 16-bit machines came, there was a new sheriff in town at Acclaim [and] he didn't like me much. He hired other groups for the 16-bit games.[1]

Other parties came into the fore as the new console generation kicked into high gear. Paul Provenzano, a producer at Acclaim, noted that the big cheese himself was interested: "Matt [Groening] got more involved. He'd seen the success of the first game but he really wanted to be a part of the second game." Provenzano remembers that Groening's input on the project "was sort of a turning point, even for Acclaim."[2] Another distinct change in Acclaim's structure was the formation of strike teams within their company who could work with external developers to develop their licensed games. Provenzano, for example, was part of the Black Team that often appears in the credits for *Simpsons* games of the era.

It certainly seemed like Acclaim was getting serious about their *Simpsons* games, but somehow I don't think "make a good *Simpsons* game" was as high a priority as "make a *Simpsons* game that looks like it belongs on 16-bit consoles so people will buy it." So they did like many a pioneer and looked to the West, far beyond Jersey's shores and into the heart of the Great Basin. There they found a developer with the chops and experience to make *Simpsons* games for the new generation of consoles: Sculptured Software.

Founded in 1984, Sculptured Software staked their claim in the wide world of game ports from other companies, first focusing on ports for computer games and then arcade-to-console ports, with *Mortal Kombat* chief among them. Sculptured Software also took on licensed games. Some well-known examples are the *Jack Nicklaus Golf* games, a long series of WWF wrestling games with Acclaim, and the exceptional *Super Star Wars* trilogy on SNES. Acclaim appeared to make a wise choice working with a company with this kind of catalogue under their belts. The technical chops for impressive 16-bit games was there, but what about the game design?

Pick your poison.

I have to admit that *Bart's Nightmare* is a flashy game. It looks like the generational leap that all players of the era expected when they purchased systems such as the Super Nintendo or Sega Genesis. The sprites were larger, more animated, and represented an ideal to which any developer of the time aspired when translating animated properties like *The Simpsons* to the pixelated screen. There was also greater variety in the art. Bart was no longer limited to being a small pixel boy in a big, open environment. The game's Windy World hub area—in which the player guides a small and relatively simplified Bart along a boring neighborhood street—probably comes closest to the visuals of previous games. The player simply walks around and jumps over enemies or uses one of several abilities such as watermelon seed shots, guided bubble gum bubbles, and a room-clearing soda burp to fight through the ever-growing hordes. Bart's animation in this area is noticeably lacking with a missing jump animation when the player leaps into the air, but it oddly fits into the hub's surreal atmosphere.

The environment also gets packed with more strange enemies over time, including flying saxophones, walking television sets, and dream versions of Principal Skinner and Lisa, and they look and sound just as weird as the rest of it. As described by Chris Antista in the interview with Paul Provenzano on the *Talking Simpsons* podcast, "It is David Lynchian in its presentation of dreams."[3] What may seem like haphazard level design may in fact be a stroke of creative genius. Provenzano recalls:

> The original concepts for *Bart's Nightmare* were kind of surreal. The first thing I saw was, maybe everybody calls it that, but we called it Windy World... And the licensing person at Fox was like, "What is going on?!"... It came from the mind of a designer who... was incredibly gifted, but also deeply troubled by any criticism or critique. And it just stayed kind of weird.[4]

The most interesting area may be the least interesting part of the game in terms of gameplay, but mastery of the hub world is essential to surviving to the end of the game. It requires collecting items and overcoming enemies in a kind of grind that rivals the most challenging RPGs. If the player loses in one of the nightmare levels, they are returned to the Windy World hub to continue the search for homework pages. The truth is that I had no clue what to do on the hub until I actually read the game manual, which is a sign that something went wrong in the design phase of the game. *Bart's Nightmare* is hardly the kind of game that requires that kind of complexity.

Ultimately, the hub's purpose was to serve as an overly complicated level select menu. Wandering through the Windy World leads to fluttering sheets of paper that Bart can hop onto, which then leads to another scene with two doors, and this is where the real game begins. It's the six nightmare levels that really show off the technical prowess of the game. Previous games heavily relied on asset reuse to efficiently construct their characters and worlds. Bart's character sprite in the first level of *Bart vs. the Space Mutants* was the same as the last. The aliens of one level looked just like the aliens in all other levels. Other games such as *Bart vs. the World* included a bonus costume or two, but the mandate of the day was generally to be as efficient as possible for the sake of time and memory limitations. The exponential leap in processor speed and memory allowed 16-bit consoles to simply do and show more than the previous generation. In the case of *Bart's Nightmare*, it allowed each level to feature unique art and gameplay that went beyond what players had experienced in past games.

That spicy nacho breath.

No one level plays like another. The Bartzilla levels behind the green door feature Bart as a *Godzilla* parody with relatively simple goals. Drawing comparisons to the future success of such auto-runner games as *Temple Run* from 2011, the first phase involves a giant-sized Bart sprite automatically walking along an urban landscape, destroying everything in his path. Each button, including the directional pad, performs a different action designed to attack a different part of the screen. This is sometimes just for destroying buildings that are out of reach, but it also serves as a defense strategy against the legions of jets, helicopters, and tanks that frequently appear. It's necessary to destroy them because Bartzilla can be killed before completing the destruction objective and then getting shrunk down for the next phase: climbing a skyscraper. They figured we got *Godzilla*, why not *King Kong*? Cover your kaiju bases, that's what I say.

The climbing phase presents a vertical scrolling section in which Bart must avoid objects dropped by inhabitants of a skyscraper as well as the hovering menace of Momthra, who must be avoided by dodging high or low and clinging onto the gutter pipes on either side of the building. All obstacles cause Bartzilla to fall down a few floors, and too many falls leads to Bartzilla falling off the screen and losing a life. Bartzilla's only defense is an electric shock attack, but it doesn't help much with the common obstacles. Eventually the building narrows and obstacles disappear, leaving only Bartzilla and his ancient nemesis, Homer Kong. Not to be confused with King Homer as featured in the "Treehouse of Horror II" episode from 1993, the Homer Kong of Bart's nightmare actually made it to the top of the building and waits to punch Bartzilla in his fat green face. The player has to carefully dodge his attacks but remain close enough to shock him when he reaches down for the swipe.

Consider yourself pacified.

The next nightmare is the Temple of Maggie, a strange riff on *Indiana Jones* in which the player moves along a series of columns in a *Q-Bert*-like fashion. Each column is pressed further into the fiery depths each time the player lands on it, requiring the player to judge their next move wisely lest they die in the pit. Additional obstacles appear in the form of a blue devil that hops around on the columns, a pterodactyl swooping down to pick up eggs, and a Maggie statue's pacifier waiting to knock Bart into the hellfire. Bart isn't completely at their mercy; he can wield a whip to fend some of the obstacles. He can also collect some of the pterodactyl's eggs before they carry them off, with each egg serving as an extra life to try again if Bart takes the plunge. Survive the temple and an altar holding a sheet of homework is the player's reward. The level must be completed again in a slightly more difficult variation to obtain the second sheet of homework and be done with the temple's tribulations.

Bartman's nightmare continues with a level based on that most classic of genres, the shoot-em-up, or SHMUP. The SHMUP is characterized by a character or machine moving through an automatically scrolling level while dodging enemies and their bullets, and also firing back at them. This level takes that foundation and adds an overlay of Bartman fighting off various characters from *The Simpsons* television show, in addition to dodging other hazards like killer paper planes and radioactive clouds. Bartman's slingshot fires rocks at a rapid clip but not in a straight line. Instead, the designers added some physics to the equation by having the rocks fall toward the bottom of the screen in an arc, and the player can hold the fire button to vary the distance they can reach. Sometimes this allows for creative positioning of Bartman on the screen for getting the maximum number of rocks to hit an opponent, but it can be a pain for other enemies that dive in low and can only be attacked by flying back up to the top of the screen. The level is ultimately one long SHMUP-fest that ends with a confrontation against Mr. Burns in a biplane. It's a repetitive battle like most of them. Personally, I think the mid-level boss fight against a drunk Barney atop a pink elephant is the most inspired boss enemy in the entire game, and perhaps all *Simpsons* games?

Look out, look out, pink elephants shoot your brain.

Now let's retreat from the beautiful skies and drop into the claustrophobic true nightmare of the Itchy & Scratchy levels. It's not the first time the Simpsons would explore the idea—more or less this same level appeared in *Bart's House of Weirdness* on PC, and the television show would send Bart and Lisa into the world of animated violence in "The Terror of Tiny Toon" segment from "Treehouse of Horror IX" in 1998. And of course there are entire games in which the player just kills Scratchy over and over again. Most attempts at a send-up of animated cartoon violence unfortunately fall flat for presenting the idea too literally. They don't make fun of cartoon violence, they merely regurgitate it. Such is the case with Itchy & Scratchy in *Bart's Nightmare*. The player guides Bart through a series of rooms in a Simpson house full of hazards in the form of the eponymous cartoon characters and other creepy household terrors. The player is initially presented with a mallet to use against the enemies but can also discover a plunger gun, bazooka, and fire extinguisher to fight them off. The gameplay consists of killing Itchy & Scratchy ad nauseam until some required threshold is hit, at which point the player may proceed to the next room to do it all over again. There are a couple of enemies that may be considered bosses, such as the giant furnace that shoots out animate fire balls. And... that's really it. This violent merry-go-round continues until the player unlocks one sheet of homework, then it repeats to unlock a second. It may be the least interesting part of the game.

Finally, and perhaps appropriately, we have Bart's Bloodstream. This single level presents Bart as a scuba diver in his own blood, free to float around from one corner of the screen to the others. Blood platelets cover the screen but only serve as background to the core action: the war between Bart and the viruses that clog his bloodstream. Bart's only defense against the viruses is to shove his air pump into them and blow them up until, well, they blow up. The viruses come in multiple forms but are all out to attack Bart before he can accomplish his goal of releasing the homework sheet that appears at the top of the screen. While it is visible early on, the force field around the sheet prevents Bart from grabbing it. This is where this level's most important character makes his appearance: Smilin' Joe Fission. This one-note character from the educational film at the Springfield Nuclear Power Plant never appears on the show again and only shows up in this one video game, reminding us that nuclear energy is "our no longer misunderstood friend."[5] His main function here isn't to educate but to pick at the force field each time Bart touches him, like some bizarre relay race that isn't all that out of place in this topsy turvy mad house of a game. Each assault by Smilin' Joe Fission weakens the force field until the homework sheet is eventually freed and Bart can go pick it up.

It's like Home Alone but murdery.

One final strange aspect of this already strange game is a dearth of sound. There are sound effects and sound clips of Bart's and other characters' voices for good measure, but music and ambient sound are surprisingly scarce. Of the game's six main levels, three are without any music at all, with just a few bits of ambience and attack sound effects to fill the soundscape. It's a notable omission and one that carries forward the poor musical reputation of the *Simpsons* games of the nineties.

Grading the game's sound.

Bart's Nightmare was initially released on SNES in 1992, then on Sega Genesis in 1993. Apart from a few minor user interface tweaks and some differences in music due to hardware limitations, it's essentially the same game. Same Windy World hub, same nightmares, same beginning to a 16-bit era that saw *The Simpsons* achieve those terrifying lows, dizzying highs, and creamy middles.

Notes

1. "Indie Gamer Chick Talks To The Amazing Garry Kitchen About Bart vs The Space Mutants"

(Twitter, 2020). Archived by James Kinsella on realotakugamer.com. Retrieved 19 March 2021.

2. Bob Mackey, Henry Gilbert, and Chris Antista, "Talking Simpsons Interviews Paul Provenzano," *Talking Simpsons* (Patreon, 2017). Retrieved 2 April 2018.

3. Ibid.

4. Ibid.

5. "Homer's Odyssey," *The Simpsons* (Fox Television, 1990). Directed by Wes Archer and written by Jay Kogen and Wallace Wolodarsky.

Chapter 8: The Hulking Hunks

Bart vs. the Juggernauts – November 1992

The Game Boy was the perfect handheld gaming device. Bring it and a few game cartridges along and you're all set for those long road trips in the back seat. But with so many choices at a relatively low price, it could be a challenge to limit the number of games to bring along. Nintendo standbys like *Mario Land*, *Link's Awakening*, and *Metroid II* were all but guaranteed, but why not try some funky new game? That is where the *Simpsons* titles on Game Boy come in. They were *other* Game Boy games, recognizable with their big yellow visages on the box but always a toss-up in terms of gameplay. Will it be good or will it be crap? Kids who played *Bart vs. the Juggernauts* may have been pleasantly surprised.

If chess was a form of execution.

Acclaim continued running roughshod over the *Simpsons* license. Oh, they weren't out to make bad games. That's never anybody's intention. But they were certainly out to make profitable games as cheaply as possible. In addition, with no real stake in the future of *The Simpsons* as a brand, Acclaim and its developers often influenced the games they made in unexpected ways. The team at the *Talking Simpsons* podcast interviewed Paul Provenzano, producer at Acclaim in the mid-nineties, and he recalls Acclaim's modus operandi during those heady days:

> No matter how much direction you gave them, it
> changed the way *The Simpsons* were presented.

That just is a function of different people with different ideas... It wasn't tied to any TV line, or storyline, it wasn't tied to anything in terms of their [Fox's] marketing goals. But for us, it was what can we put in a game or what can we adapt to a game.[1]

They say there's no bad pizza, but there it is.

Such was the case in 1991, a rather big year for Imagineering Inc. Sure they released three *Simpsons* games that year alone, but they developed an additional six games with wide-ranging licenses such as *Attack of the Killer Tomatoes*, *Barbie*, and a *Jeopardy!* game. These games were all published by a variety of publishers, with

Imagineering's parent company, Absolute Entertainment, left out of the publishing part of Imagineering's projects. This prolific output carried forward into 1992 with no less than ten Imagineering games appearing in stores. 1992 would also be the final year of Imagineering's involvement with the *Simpsons* license.

The first of their final two games was a Game Boy title unlike the previous efforts. While *Escape from Camp Deadly* was designed to be a linear platformer with basic jump and shoot gameplay, *Bart vs. the Juggernauts* was a selection of mini games in which Bart competes against hulking men and women known as Juggernauts. The impetus for this game was a rather quaint meeting of minds in a parking lot. As Provenzano recalls:

> I remember it was a sunny day and the five of us were sitting in a parking lot in Oyster Bay, because Acclaim had outgrown Oyster Bay and we just had no room anywhere. We kept renting buildings. The downtown of Oyster Bay was hosting Acclaim all over the place. So one of the parking lots, we're sitting there and somebody had seen American Ninjas. "What about this?" And it just became that little Game Boy game, which had very little to do with *The Simpsons*.[2]

This allowed Imagineering's game designers—Bill Jannott, Dan Kitchen, and Barry Marx—to structure the game as groups of selectable events, giving the player a bit more freedom in how they approach the game. This is the same approach used in their previous NES game, *Bart vs. the World*, as well as the 16-bit games from Sculptured Software.

It's interesting to see that the company's key figures—David Crane and Garry Kitchen—stop appearing in the credits. It's understandable for the heads of a growing company to get away from contributing directly to the products under their purview, but I also have to wonder if the *Simpsons* titles simply became less significant parts of the company's bottom line. After all, they weren't working on the 16-bit future of the *Simpsons* video games, since companies like Sculptured Software and BITS Ltd. won those contracts. It's not tough to speculate that these *Simpsons* games became contractual obligations for Imagineering to knock out as quickly as possible.

This feels familiar...

As contractual obligations go, this is a pretty good effort. I have previously noted that these early *Simpsons* games had little or none of the show's trademark humor and wit. Not that anyone expected video games of this era to pack in jokes the way they did on a sitcom (unless you were a fan of LucasArts...[3]), but a game based on *The Simpsons* really needed to start with the writing. It would take another five years for a dialogue-driven game to appear on shelves in the form of *Virtual Springfield* (Chapter 14), which was nothing short of a celebration of the television show, its characters, and the entire town of Springfield. But until then, this humble Game Boy game was somehow the best effort to date. The jokes come in the form of commentary between the two hosts of the Juggernauts broadcast: news anchor Kent Brockman and psychologist Dr. Marvin Monroe. There are some half a dozen exchanges between Monroe and Brockman in which they comment on Bart's success or failure in each event, and some of those are actually funny enough to draw a smile. It's entirely secondary to the gameplay and the designers could've gotten away with just presenting the events with no commentary whatsoever, but this extra writing really does help elevate the game. There are also introductory bits of dialogue from well-established characters from the show, further proving that the designers of this game had a better grasp on the license than whoever decided that random space aliens are the only characters who should speak in a *Simpsons* game. That it all appears in a Game Boy game of all platforms makes it even more of an oddity, and it's something few *Simpsons* games would even attempt.

It speaks!

But the interstitial dialogue scenes are merely set dressing for the game's core gameplay: four rounds of gameplay portrayed as weekly events in which Bart faces off against the titular Juggernauts. This theme is lifted directly from nineties reality show staples such as *American Gladiators* and *American Ninja Warrior*, shows in which amateur competitors signed up to compete in contests of strength and agility against a cast of muscleheads with names like Nitro, Gemini, and Ice. The characters in *Bart vs. the Juggernauts* are appropriately more brutish and menacing, providing ample threat for a ten-year old kid. Each week of events is merely a narrative reason to group events into levels and gate the player's progress. There is no concept of lives and health in this game. Instead, Bart accumulates a certain amount of money in each event, depending on how well the player performs the task at hand. Each week of events requires the player to reach a certain threshold of money: $10,000, $26,000, $52,000, and finally $100,000. Players are allowed to overshoot and their money carries over from one week to the next, which is good because sometimes the winning margin can be razor thin. Players who win all events in a week may also proceed to a bonus event for extra money in which Bart drops weights on a Juggernaut's weight bar within a time limit.

KO'S

D'S

Hits TIMER Hits
84

Don't worry, the nuclear waste will catch him.

But enough jibber-jabber, let's get to the main event. The game's seven events are introduced over the course of the game and sometimes appear more than once, giving players an opportunity to replay past events with a little more experience under their belt. The first event is Dr. Marvin Monroe's Hop, Skip and Fry. This combo of basketball and hop scotch sees Bart jumping through a minefield of alternating electric tiles while also avoiding two continually pestering Juggernaut goons. Each pass through the field requires Bart to drop a ball in the basket and then return to pick up a new ball and try again. The other event introduced in week 1 is Capt. Murdock's

Skateboard Bash and Crash, a simple downhill slalom on a skateboard with a ramp at the end, and the final obstacle a shielded Juggernaut that must be taken out with a well-aimed kick to the head or torso. If the player survives to week 2 they'll take on the challenge of the Nuclear Power Plant Bop 'Till You Drop. Based on the *American Gladiators* event called Joust, Bart must use his padded bow staff to defend against and attack a Juggernaut. Each character attempts to knock the other into the pool of nuclear goo below. The similar Moe's Tavern Shove Fest requires Bart to shove a Juggernaut off the edge of a wrestling mat by using moves such as kicks, head butts, and of course shoves aplenty.

The challenge increases in the latter part of the game as Herman's Military Minefield Mayhem appears. This challenging combat simulator requires Bart to navigate the skies in a parachute while dodging Juggernaut projectiles, then a minefield with barbed wire dotted along the way. This one requires fine motor skills and a modicum or two of patience. The Krustyland Hammer Slammer is seemingly a respite with its simple layout, but keeping the Juggernauts from reaching the ground can become a harried exercise in juggling. Fortunately, a Juggernaut juice powerup gives Bart the strength to knock one of the Juggernauts out of contention and is definitely not a steroid cocktail. Finally, we come to the most traditional of video game events: a platformer stage! The Kwik-E-Mart Doggie Dodge comes in at the end perhaps as a nod to the fact that almost all games of the era were entirely platformer games, but it's more likely that it made a fitting finale as the longest single event in the game. It can also be quite a challenge due to the time it takes to clear the event. Bart's objective is to navigate a labyrinthian version of the Kwik-E-Mart convenience store while dodging packs of bloodthirsty dogs. There are bones available to distract them and sausages to use as shields, and fortunately these dogs aren't the fastest and can be dodged with relative ease.

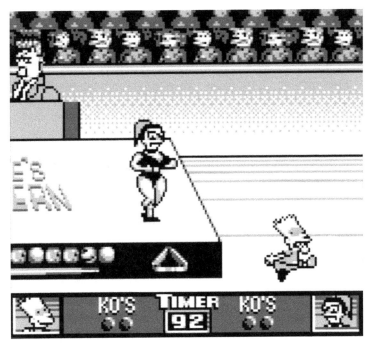

A date with Snarla would be fine by me.

All of these events are presented in simplified Game Boy graphics but still look quite good for 160 by 144 pixel resolution. The music is also a surprise, composed by Mark Van Hecke, the same composer from previous Imagineering titles. I think it's mostly the fact that it's not just the *Simpsons* theme playing ad nauseam.

My memories of the game were betrayed by the fact that they were mixed in with so many other *Simpsons* games. Reviewed on its own merits, this game far outpaces the previous attempts on Game Boy and rivals any of the *Simpsons* titles on NES. It only raised the ancient wisdom: when in doubt, do like the *American Gladiators*.

Notes

1. Bob Mackey, Henry Gilbert, and Chris Antista, "Talking Simpsons Interviews Paul Provenzano," *Talking Simpsons* (Patreon, 2017). Retrieved 2 April 2018.
2. Ibid.
3. PCMag Staff and Chloe Albanesius, "LucasArts Hall of Fame: Our Favorite Games" (PCMag, 2013). Retrieved 20 March 2021.

Chapter 9: The Radioactive Dumps

Bartman Meets Radioactive Man - January 1993

At this point in the book I get to reveal my origin story. Why video games, why *The Simpsons*, why *Simpsons* video games? I was in college and I suddenly had to make decisions. Who would I become in this new world? Well, it turns out I'd really lean into that ol' Internet, and in particular the video game message boards at the GameFAQs website.[1] I began as a regular boarder (in the parlance of the time) and realized that I could contribute more than just pithy college-aged quips like "peez out." GameFAQs was also a repository of those titular FAQs and walkthroughs, and I soon noticed that my longtime interest in *The Simpsons* was represented in that vast digital archive. There were so many *Simpsons* video games, far beyond what I could have conceived. I missed most of those games but found a chance to read about them and, more importantly, play them. And once I started playing them I couldn't help but notice that very few of them had walkthroughs. It was a calling! It was momentous! It was... something to focus on at a strange time of my life. I considered my approach through that first semester of college and started writing in January of 2002.

That first fateful writing project became a walkthrough for this game: *Bartman Meets Radioactive Man*. And let me tell you, it's been a weird and amazing nineteen years. Remember, kids, you too can pursue your nerdy interests for no pay at all!

A dog day afternoon.

It may have been the beginning for me, but little did I know that *Bartman Meets Radioactive Man* represented the end of an era. Imagineering Inc. kicked off the *Simpsons* games on home consoles when they developed *Bart vs. the Space Mutants*, and this fifth *Simpsons* title from the company—released nearly two years after the first game—would be their last *Simpsons* collaboration with

Acclaim. As we discovered in Chapter 7, executive turnover led to the end of Imagineering's involvement.

And this last hurrah on the NES is a strange one. Looking through the credits and some of the developers' websites, it's interesting to see that David Crane (who appeared in Chapters 2 and 3) doesn't list *Bartman Meets Radioactive Man* in the credits on his website.[2] Garry Kitchen only lists *Bart vs. the Space Mutants*.[3] I have to speculate that this game was a contractual obligation by this point, meant to wring a few more dollars out of the NES. It also has the sense of a game relegated to a B-team at Absolute Entertainment—parent company of Imagineering—while the company's big names moved on to bigger things. This game's credits are also notable for the variety of new names that weren't included in previous *Simpsons* titles, including a dedicated team from Acclaim themselves, who were previously not credited very often in the games. Commenting on a perceived drop in quality with the controls, designer Dan Kitchen notes:

> Unfortunately, it's due to a different programming team. By the time *Radioactive Man* was in development, the lead programmers were busy on larger titles and we put less experienced guys on the game. It was a business decision I wish we hadn't done.[4]

Later that year, Imagineering's staff would be absorbed back into Absolute Entertainment and Imagineering would cease to exist, ending Imagineering's short but prolific place in the annals of game development history.

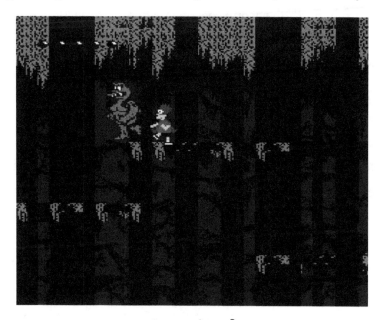

Care to dance?

Audiences familiar with *The Simpsons* might have recognized Bart's heroic alter ego in 1992. The mantle of "Bartman" first appeared not as a costumed character but as the title of a pop song called "Do the Bartman" from the 1990 album *The Simpsons Sing the Blues*. Written by music producer Bryan Loren and with vocal support from Michael Jackson, the single climbed to the top of several countries' song charts. The song blew up in the U.S. in 1991 when the Brad Bird-directed music video for *Do the Bartman* took over MTV and received a nomination at the MTV Awards.

That same year, the writers for the show ran with the concept of Bartman by briefly introducing Bart's heroic alter-ego in the second season episode, "Three Men and a Comic Book." The character's cowl and cape are a clear reference to Batman, who was back in pop culture's fickle grip after the release of Tim Burton's *Batman* in 1989. The joke in the show is that any person wearing a superhero costume can enter a comic book convention for free, but they don't recognize Bart's homemade costume. This episode also marks the full introduction of Radioactive Man, the World War II-era comic hero who Bart and his friends idolize. Both Bartman and Radioactive Man would appear again in various forms on the show and enjoy full prints runs through Matt Groening's Bongo Comics imprint, as well as appearances in various video games. Many a game designer looking for a way to give Bart more advanced powers would find an easy crutch in Bartman.

Ain't no party like a limbo party.

Bartman Meets Radioactive Man arrived during a transition period in the video game industry. 8-bit consoles—and game design informed by the limits of that technology—were on their way out. The world had already seen a more diverse approach to *Simpsons* game design with *Bart's Nightmare* on SNES and Sega Genesis, and along comes this relatively simple action-platformer, on outdated hardware, featuring characters that were used to poke fun at comics and their fans. Unlike the show's writers, the game designers took a self-serious approach in designing a quest in which Bart must don his cape and cowl to rescue Radioactive Man from his imprisonment in a place called the Limbo Zone. It's *The Neverending Story* meets *Superman* with none of the trademark humor from the television show.

Bartman made brief appearances as a bonus power-up in *Bart vs. the World* (Chapter 4) and the lead persona in the flying shooter level of *Bart's Nightmare* (Chapter 7), as well as later releases such as *The Simpsons Game* (Chapter 22), but this is the first and only time that Bartman is the star in a video game. Dan Kitchen recalls how that came about:

> We finished *The World* and then Acclaim approached us for yet another *Simpsons* title. This time they wanted us to focus on Bart's alter-ego, Bartman. They wanted this to appear as an interactive comic book.5

The designers leveraged the persona to extend Bart's abilities and make things more interesting for the player, with some success and some mediocrity as a result. For starters, the designers continued their exploration of the action-platformer genre and avoided further attempts at the overly intricate puzzles and inventory management from *Bart vs. the Space Mutants*. They also gave Bart an ability that was somehow missing until this game: melee attacks! The player can press the attack button once for a punch attack, or two and three times to execute a combo attack. It's a small but significant improvement that adds to the action element of the game. Bartman also has what the game manual calls mighty-powers, which are limited to the currently assigned power-up. This type of limitation can feel annoying when a different power-up is desired but is a standard design introduced in action-shooters like *Contra*. The most common power-up is the laser beams, granting Bartman the ability to shoot lasers from his eyes. The cold breath power-up grants fewer shots but they are more powerful and actually required to progress through certain levels. These two mighty-powers are available through power-ups scattered throughout the game and are sometimes just available by default. While they're not innovative by 1992, they definitely were a leap forward for *Simpsons* games on 8-bit systems. Bart can also pick up a temporary tornado power-up that grants invincibility and allows Bartman to charge through enemies without a care, and the temporary flying power-up that first appeared in *Bart vs. the World* returns here to give Bartman the ability to fly in the platformer levels.

If you say so.

Gameplay is spread out across three chapters consisting of two to four levels a piece followed by a boss fight. The fourth and final chapter skips more levels in favor of a final battle with the brain in a tank known as Brain-O the Magnificent. Of course the bosses aren't the only enemies. Each level comes with its own gallery of rogues, from the tiniest rats to giant crabs and a wild assortment of goons. Enemy design isn't the most inspired, with their attacks limited to the usual patrols across platforms and simple projectiles. And while their patterns are simple, enemies are frequent and dangerous enough to make the game a tough trek for any player.

Here we get to a baffling choice in level design. The game's main three chapters are comprised of various levels that implement new mechanics and challenges for the player... just not right away. The first level, for example, is a journey through a long and monotonous junkyard with simple enemies and many, many pits to avoid. It has little in the way of new mechanics and seems designed to really just introduce players to the core gameplay. The problem is it's so boring compared to later levels. The second level of chapter 1 is almost worse with its sewer pipe labyrinth that offers no interesting environments or challenges, simply another long slog and too many dead-ends. There's an old tenet of game design that proposes the best way to engage players is to come out strong with your best stuff and end it the same way, leaving the saggy middle to guide the player along to the exciting conclusion. This game doesn't follow that. The first two levels are just so off-putting. The third level and boss fight against Swamp Hag of the first chapter turn it around by introducing a flying level and interesting platforming challenges, but I have to wonder how many players were willing to trudge through the beginning of the game to get there.

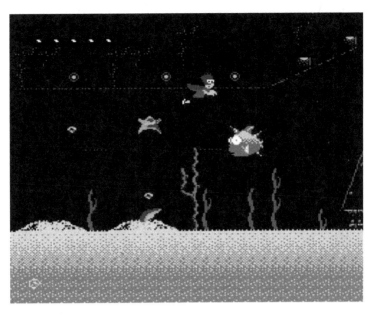

Darling it's better, down where it's wetter.

The second chapter through Dr. Crab's underwater lair ramps up the interesting gameplay by allowing the player to swim freely as they navigate the tunnels and gullies, then a section with a spotlight looking to shoot Bartman as he passes in front of the crosshair. The final part of chapter 2 is not quite as fun with its return to rote platforming, but it's bookended by some of the best parts of the game. The final battle against Dr. Crab is probably the coolest boss fight. Instead of attacking directly, Bartman holds up his fist to punch Dr. Crab as he descends for a flying lunge onto Bartman's head. Several of these hits cause Dr. Crab to crash through the wall, after which the player must repeat the attacks to defeat him for good.

Chapter 3 takes place in the hellish caverns of Lava Man's lair. This level is generally focused on platforming but introduces a vertical descent element that's kinda neat. Bartman can extend his arms to slow down his falls through lava tubes, which is just different enough to make it interesting. The second level takes place in another labyrinth through a ruined city, but unlike the dreadful sewer of chapter 1, this labyrinth leads the player on a search through various doorways and tunnels to hunt down the exit door. The environments are also far more interesting than the drab green walls of that sewer. The chapter eventually ends with a confrontation against Lava Man himself. This battle harkens back to the Swamp Hag fight with the use of cold breaths to freeze falling obstacles. This time, freezing the obstacles is the only way to hit Lava Man as he appears in the lava below.

With Radioactive Man free and only one enemy left to fight, the two heroes team up to take on the mastermind behind his imprisonment: Brain-O the Magnificent. Bartman can fire laser beams at the tank to no effect, but if the player hits the tank at the right angle and waits for Radioactive Man to fly overhead, the laser beams will rebound off Radioactive Man and hit Brain-O's soft spot. It's a long battle and not that interesting a boss fight, but anyone who has survived this long will be glad to get it over with. The ending is similarly banal, although players of the prototype version of the game available online will find a distinctly different (and far better) ending.[6]

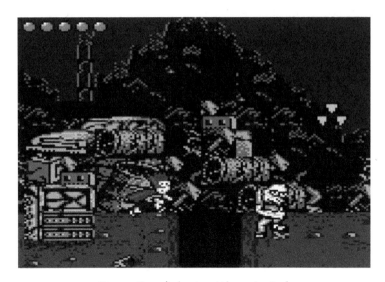

Game Gear's just getting started.

The age of mass porting was at an end for *Simpsons* games when the NES version shipped in 1993 and the game only appeared on one additional platform: the Sega Game Gear. It was a mostly faithful port from Teeny Weeny Games that slightly improved the visuals but of course squished everything down onto the tiny handheld screen. This required the developers to limit the player view and implement a camera shift in which the camera moved toward the direction the player was facing, and even moved down when Bartman ducks so the player can see enemies or obstacles below. The one major gameplay change was in the spotlight level of chapter 3, where the player must avoid a spotlight and target in an otherwise pitch black labyrinth. The Game Gear version of this level simply requires the player to swim into light bulbs scattered around the area in order to keep the level lit. Otherwise, there were a few notable visual changes like enemy costume colors changing from blue to red, or extra characters appearing in the ending screens. This late port of the game (it didn't ship until about March of 1994) arrived amid a couple of Game Boy releases and *Virtual Bart* on Sega Genesis and SNES, so nearly at the end of the first rush of *Simpsons* game releases. And somehow, this wouldn't be the last *Simpsons* game on Game Gear.

Notes

1. "GameFAQs Community - SubSane" (GameFAQs, 2021). Retrieved 20 March 2021.
2. David Crane, "Softwareology" (2021). Retrieved 20 March 2021.
3. Garry Kitchen, "Product History" (2021). Retrieved 20 March 2021.
4. "Indie Gamer Chick Talks To Dan Kitchen About Bart vs The World/Bartman Meets Radioactive Man" (Twitter, 2020). Archived by James Kinsella on realotakugamer.com. Retrieved 20 March 2021.
5. Ibid.
6. "Proto:The Simpsons: Bartman Meets Radioactive Man (NES)" (The Cutting Room Floor, 2021). Retrieved 20 March 2021.

Chapter 10: The Beanstalk Tolls for Thee

Bart and the Beanstalk - February 1994

I wasn't a dedicated collector as a kid. There were a few flirtations with pogs and comic trading cards, but those were brief and tied to schoolyard fads. The closest to collecting that I'd come is buying video games, but even then I traded away games without a moment's hesitation and was happy to buy just the cartridge or disc if it was cheaper. Old things were nice, sure, but there were so many *new* things. This changed when I finally became interested in *Star Wars* in 1997. Lucasfilm had just released the special edition versions of the original trilogy and it suddenly clicked that this sci-fi space opera was pretty cool. I was also a teenager by then with more disposable income than I'd ever had as a child. So I watched the movies... read the books of the expanded universe... bought the toys... and played the video games. And because I was already especially interested in video games, that was the category of collectible that stuck with me the most. I hunted down *Star Wars* video games from the past and present, and buying games complete with box and manual suddenly mattered. Those physical artifacts just lent a certain something to my enjoyment of the stories. It was the genesis of my collector brain.

I began with *Star Wars* and other video games all through high school but I tuned into my *Simpsons* collector persona in college. It was light collecting I'd say, buying whatever games were released in stores at the time and occasionally picking up oddities on eBay. But I didn't have a completionist mindset. I was happy to download ROMs and cracked builds of old games on PC to play them all. I have no idea what some of the more rare *Simpsons* games even cost back when I began in the early aughts because I never bothered to look them up. It's certain they would've been a lot cheaper than they are now.

And so we come to *Bart and the Beanstalk* on Nintendo Game Boy. I didn't own an original Game Boy until the Game Boy Pocket was in stores in the mid-nineties, and even then I only really played cornerstone games like *The Legend of Zelda: Link's Awakening* and *Pokemon Red*. Most of my Game Boy play time was in emulators on a PC. Then when I did buy a *Simpsons* Game Boy game such as *Escape from Camp Deadly*, it was only because it was so common that I couldn't avoid it. *Bart and the Beanstalk* didn't enter my radar until after I'd forgotten about *Simpsons* games for close to ten years and then returned in full force, ready to complete a collection I'd begun nearly twenty years before. I was surprised to see that a complete box of *Bart and the Beanstalk* was now selling for close to *three hundred* U.S. dollars. The game shipped from Acclaim at a time when the market already had nearly a dozen *Simpsons* games available. Perhaps the game sold so poorly that the first print run was the only set of copies in existence. And sure the cartridge alone sells for cheap, but who wants that? There may have been other options to obtain a copy, but complete sets appeared to be so rare that I bit that bullet and purchased it from eBay when a complete copy popped up. I'd become a fan of video series about old video games like those from journalist and video game archivist Jeremy Parish, who occasionally warns viewers of the perils of being a completionist with old game collections. I thought he'd said it in a tongue in cheek manner but now I wonder if it was a serious P.S.A...[1]

But the fact is that I do own it now. The itch has been scratched, the box sits on a shelf, and I'm left to wonder if a half-hour game with zero replay value was really worth the trouble. Consider thee warned.

THEY WERE SO
POOR, THAT ALL
THEY HAD WERE
SOME OLD DONUTS
AND A COW.

(WHAT GOOD
ARE DONUTS
WITHOUT MILK?)

No money, mo Simpsons video games.

Bart and the Beanstalk came about in the waning years of *Simpsons* games for 8-bit platforms. The Game Boy alone had already seen three releases in three years and though the Game Boy was feeling long in the tooth by 1994, it was still a platform that allowed for small-scope games with matching small budgets. Acclaim still held the *Simpsons* license and it felt like their real budgets for *Simpsons* games was going into games like *Bart's Nightmare* and *Virtual Bart*, with Game Boy and Game Gear games being churned out to bring in a few extra bucks. *Bart and the Beanstalk* was the first of these extra buck games.

Acclaim turned back to the UK to find a developer for *Bart and the Beanstalk*, ultimately choosing to work with a developer called Software Creations out of Manchester, England. It may seem strange for Acclaim to veer off and find a new developer after years of working with Imagineering and Sculptured Software, but producer Paul Provenzano recalls that it was just business: "Acclaim, at the time, worked exclusively with outside developers. It was a pretty standard list of guys that we just rotate around to various projects." So Acclaim was in the market for a new developer to add to their stable.[2]

Like many of the development companies we've seen so far, Software Creations began as a developer of computer games in the eighties before pivoting to licensed games across a wider variety of platforms in the nineties. In fact, games based on popular comic and movie licenses became a key part of Software Creations' business. Other notable titles from Software Creations that shipped the same year as this game include *Spider-Man and Venom: Maximum Carnage* and *The Tick*, both colorful punch-fests on 16-bit consoles that were fun to look at but difficult to play. They were quite different from *Bart and the Beanstalk*. For one, those games had sizable teams of fifteen to twenty-five people. *Bart and the Beanstalk* appears to have had a core team of a handful of people with other developers pitching in where necessary. The size of the team doesn't dictate the quality of the game, but it certainly shows that the budget was not high. There are some shared names between all of Software Creations credits but one name from *Bart and the Beanstalk* stood out: lead producer and designer Brian Ullrich. He had only worked at Software Creations for a few years but had been credited in the same role on other notable titles like *Zoda's Revenge: StarTropics II* and *Plok*. It looks like *Bart and the Beanstalk* was headed up by Ullrich with a small team of people to help knock out this quick project on Game Boy. The limited team size and budget would be reflected in the game itself.

A humble beginning... and middle and ending.

The previous *Simpsons* game on Game Boy, *Bart vs. the Juggernauts*, was a surprising and refreshing entry in the series. It was a mini game collection at its core but the change in format and extra bits of funny dialogue felt like an elevation of the game beyond the platform-fests we've seen for most of this book, which makes sense when the same developer is tasked with making the same game over and over again. They were looking for a change.

So with that in mind we get *Bart and the Beanstalk*, which sees a new developer take on the license for another joke-free platformer bereft of any of the show's charm and humor. As the title implies, Bart takes the place of Jack in the fairy tale of the boy who gets swindled for a pile of magic beans that grow into a massive beanstalk to the clouds. The boy climbs the beanstalk, steals a golden goose away from a giant living in a castle, and returns to his family as a hero. The *Simpsons* version of this story is much the same, with short storybook scenes utilizing text and the occasional illustration to advance the story. It fits the fairy tale nature of the game but is also clearly a budgetary choice to avoid pricey animation and cutscenes. It is somewhat amusing to see *Simpsons* characters like Homer and Mr. Burns take on the roles of the story's characters, but it amounts to some vandal Simpsonizing the illustrations in a storybook.

Psst, kid, want a Game Boy game?

The gameplay is the simplest platforming and shooting you can imagine. The player guides Bart along a series of platforms while using a slingshot and other weapons to fight off a cadre of giant insects and rodents. The movement physics and animation are unfortunately stiff and not the most fun character controls, but serviceable for the game. Bart can also climb vines, bounce on clouds and springs, and the final level introduces a downward slalom in which Bart parachutes down along the beanstalk and avoids obstacles. These small movement changes introduce welcome variety in a game full of platform jumps and a surprising difficulty curve.

The first level of *Bart and the Beanstalk* has a similar problem as *Bart vs. the Space Mutants* but for different reasons. *Bart vs. the Space Mutants* introduced the game with an obtuse design that incorporated adventure game elements and a challenging gauntlet of enemies, discouraging most players from continuing further into the game. *Bart and the Beanstalk* opens by doubling down on the gauntlet approach with a vertical slog along a treacherous beanstalk full of enemies, spikes, and precarious jumps over death pits. It's a cruel start and the few players who purchased the game back in 1994 were undoubtedly ready to quit before they ever reached the giant beetle boss at the top.

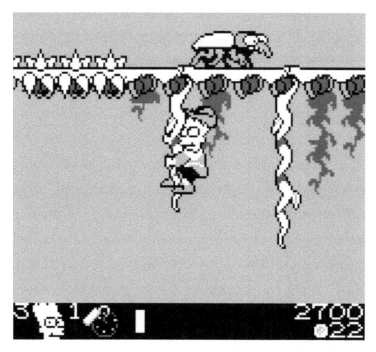

Hang on, there's only twenty more minutes of game to go!

Those who did make it beyond the first level and the subsequent tromp through the clouds arrived at the giant's castle, which is the best part of the game. The three middle levels all feature giant-sized silverware and miscellany that do far more to kickstart the imagination than the previous levels, though they feature the same gameplay. This part of the game contains the player's primary goals beyond the gold coins collected in every level: the living harp and golden goose. These macguffins are right out of the fairy tale and provide more interesting objectives than "get to the end of the level," though that's where they are found. There is also a short but amusing portion where Bart jumps across lumps of food floating in a soup while collecting more gold coins and dodging a salt shaker's bombardment from above.

The final two levels cover Bart's escape from the castle with his stolen booty. First is an auto-scrolling section in which the player guides Bart back through the cloud area but at a faster pace, striving to stay to the left side of the screen lest the giant reach and crush them. It's a high-pressure chase and probably more fun than the initial slow-paced infiltration level. The final level is a similar mirror flip of the first level with Bart floating down along a vertically scrolling map. Beanstalk platforms come back to haunt the player one last time by serving as barriers to be avoided before the player is trapped by the top of the screen. The developers made sure to provide a path of gold coins to help navigate back to the ground, where an axe to chop down the beanstalk lies in wait.

A spit take in video game form.

If you did the math, that's seven levels at five to ten minutes a piece. Novice players may find their playthrough a bit lengthier but it's simply quite a short game. And the aforementioned rote platforming makes it feel like a smaller slice of the same game *Simpsons* fans had received for years. But the game does have a certain vibe that I appreciate. *Bart and the Beanstalk* actually feels like the closest they get to the *Super Mario Bros.* series. By abandoning any sense of logic from the *Simpsons* universe and dwelling in a surreal place where Homer and Mr. Burns's faces can be slapped onto beetles and clouds, the game becomes a kind of fever dream, matching the nightmarish tone of the games that appeared on 16-bit platforms. It's no surprise that I'm a big fan of the show's "Treehouse of Horror" episodes, where the show accomplishes the same feat with the television series (albeit at a different level from a cheaply made Game Boy game). These nonsensical stories break open the rules of the show's characters and their universe. Bart can have psychic powers, become a vampire, or converse with the spirit in a haunted house. This game strives to also break the rules of what a *Simpsons* can be, but in a far more limited way. I can't help but think that if they'd thrown the dialogue over to a writer from the show to punch it up, the game's short length and high difficulty might have been more enjoyable than what we actually got. It's another case of failing to live up to the high bar set by outstanding source material.

Notes

1. Jeremy Parish, "Retronauts Video Works" (YouTube, 2021). Retrieved 20 March 2021.

2. Bob Mackey, Henry Gilbert, and Chris Antista, "Talking Simpsons Interviews Paul Provenzano," *Talking Simpsons* (Patreon, 2017). Retrieved 2 April 2018.

Chapter 11: The Miniature Screams

Itchy & Scratchy in Miniature Golf Madness – August 1994

Something was going on with Game Boy games from Acclaim in 1994. The previous Game Boy game in the series—*Bart and the Beanstalk*—saw a limited print run that resulted in a rarity now worth upwards of three hundred bucks. *Itchy & Scratchy in Miniature Golf Madness* is in the exact same position, with a complete box fetching between two and three hundred dollars on eBay. As we'll learn, the value has nothing to do with the gameplay.

Being only ten years old when the game was released, and not owning a Game Boy, I missed this game completely. So in this regard I was like most people who didn't pay attention to its existence until their collector vice prompted them to seek it out. I own a copy now but I first learned about it when I seeked it out many years later in my quest to write walkthroughs for all *Simpsons* games. One curious aspect of writing a walkthrough for a game is how easily it is forgotten. I have few lasting memories from the many walkthroughs I wrote, and it's simply because writing a walkthrough is work. Not in the building a fence sense of work, but just the way you approach the game. You analyze it, break it down, and write what are essentially instructions for making your way through the software. That doesn't leave much room to take in the experience as a player would in a more natural setting. And so I can say I completed *Itchy & Scratchy in Miniature Golf Madness*, but I barely remembered the experience. It wasn't until I actually played the game without the aid of save states many years later that I saw the wonder of what they had accomplished.

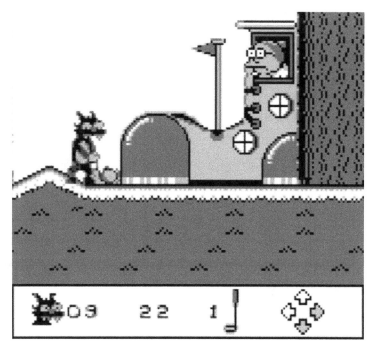

The shoe trap on hole 1 is a doozy.

The year 1994 marked the last gasp of Acclaim's firm grip on the *Simpsons* license. They had just released *Bart and the Beanstalk* and would soon follow this game with *Virtual Bart*, the last big effort for a triple-A *Simpsons* game on consoles. *Itchy & Scratchy in Miniature Golf Madness* feels like more of an oddity in light of the fact that Acclaim had another Itchy & Scratchy game in the pipeline for consoles that they would release in early 1995. It's clear that someone thought games featuring Bart Simpon (or heaven forbid, the entire Simpson family) were no longer interesting enough for these side platforms. They had already sold a game featuring Krusty the clown, so why not Itchy & Scratchy? These two characters hail from the Tom and Jerry-style animated shorts featured on the show, and their myriad violent adventures seemed perfectly geared toward an era of video games in which gameplay often featured cartoony animated characters committing wanton acts of violence. A worthwhile game design in theory, but perhaps not in practice. In fact, according to producer Paul Provenzano, it was Matt Groening himself who sometimes pushed for more of the gore:

> The interesting thing about Matt being more involved is it's sort of like The Simpsons show. You know, Matt's version of The Simpsons... is kind of different than what the show evolved into being. He wanted more, like, throttling Bart, you know the early season, those kind of really over the top violent antics.[1]

As with the previous Game Boy game, Acclaim put out feelers to find a new developer for Itchy & Scratchy's first solo outing. They reached all the way out to Melbourne, Australia to work with Beam Software. The game developer was first founded in 1980 and focused on computer games, with releases such as the text adventure *The Hobbit* from 1982 and *Way of the Exploding Fist* from 1985 setting the stage for their fifteen year run as an independent success in the game industry. The company shifted to console development in 1987 and released two or three titles a year until their productivity exploded in 1990. Like many of the developers we've learned about, the company went through a period of rapid growth as 8-bit and then 16-bit consoles proliferated around the world. The company took on ports of other companies' hits—licenses such as NFL and *George Foreman's KO Boxing*—but they are perhaps best known for their adaptations of *Aussie Rules Footy* and *Shadowrun. Itchy & Scratchy in Miniature Golf Madness* stands out as the company's only *Simpsons* game, released amid eight other games from Beam Software in 1994. Ironically, that was the same year they released another game featuring a cat and mouse duo: *Tom and Jerry - Frantic Antics* for Sega Genesis.

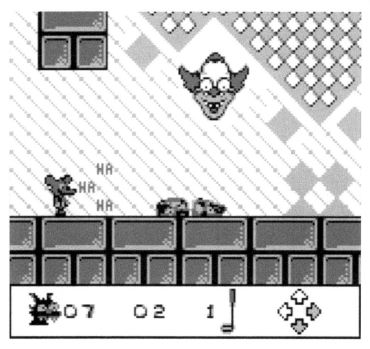

Even for a psychotic mouse, that's a jerk move.

The mid-nineties was a tumultuous period when developers were forced to adapt to a radically shifted game industry. 32- and 64-bit consoles were the new hotness and 2D side-scrolling was quickly replaced by 3D exploration as the best-selling medium. This required new skills and talent, longer development periods, and significantly increased budgets. Beam Software continued to release games independently until 1999 when the company was acquired by Infogrames and renamed Infogrames Melbourne House, beginning a period of frequent mergers and acquisitions for them.

Their one *Simpsons* game did try to change the formula by introducing a miniature golf angle to the tried-and-true 2D action-platformer, but how successful was this mix of genres? I'd say they were significantly over par.

Let's see, carry the 1, divide by the hypotenuse...

The player takes on the role of Scratchy, a black cat that is often the victim of Itchy the mouse's psychopathic pranks and assaults. It's an interesting choice to feature Scratchy as the protagonist versus an army of AI-controlled Itchys when the animated shorts on *The Simpsons* always show Itchy as the aggressor. One episode in particular—"Homer Goes to College" from season five—plays up the fact that the "Itchy & Scratchy Show" would finally show Scratchy getting Itchy. It's played up as a major television event and is leveraged as a source of comedic blue balls when the television set is accidentally shut off, depriving Bart and Lisa of the once-in-a-lifetime TV event. And then along comes Beam Software who so boldly declare, "You wanna see Scratchy kill Itchy? Here, just do it a few dozen times." Acclaim corrected this odd role switch in the next game featuring the gory duo, aptly and succinctly titled *The Itchy & Scratchy Game* (Chapter 13), which stars Itchy as the protagonist fighting off an army of Scratchys in myriad bloody ways. Of course that is a more straightforward action-platformer, with none of this game's mini golf stylings.

Of those two core tenets of the game design, the game leans heavily into the action-platformer. The game takes place over the course of nine levels, each a labyrinthian miniature golf course in which the player guides a golf ball along while avoiding or killing Itchy. He appears at specific points and attacks with all kinds of horrifying things like bats, bombs, and bazookas. Scratchy does have a limit on lives so some skill is required to ensure he doesn't die too many times. However once Itchy is removed, the course is clear for the player to whack the golf ball along. Hitting the ball involves standing at the ball and charging the typical power meter seen in classics like Nintendo's *Golf* and *Lee Carvallo's Putting Challenge*.[2]

While there are some sections that require precision putting, most of the journey through the game consists of power drives to move the ball along. The courses are also littered with obstacles such as trick doors and warp holes to slow down and confuse the player as they traverse the mazes and attempt to stay under par. Remember, this is still mini golf.

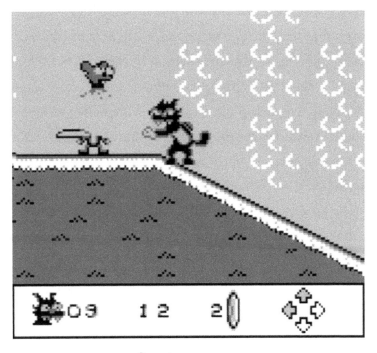

Sweet vengeance.

The Simpsons is no stranger to the world's finest miniature sport. Homer and Flanders famously carried out a cold war when their sons competed in a miniature golf tournament,[3] and Homer worked at the local miniature golf course where Bart was conceived in a miniature windmill.[4] Scoring in this game is much like regular golf, where the point is to get the ball into the hole with as few strokes of a club as possible. Like golf, each level has a par, or number of strokes that are required to reach the end of the course. The goal is to use less strokes than the par amount in order to maintain a negative value, and the lower the value the higher the score at the end. There are also aids scattered throughout the level to help lower the number of strokes. Eraser pick-ups in the levels lower the number of strokes by one for each eraser discovered, and secret holes in the environments either give Scratchy shortcuts to the end of the level or contain weapon power-ups to use against Itchy.

As in mini golf, each course has a theme, and in this case each course begins with a cringe-worthy pun like those used for episode titles on "The Itchy & Scratchy Show." The theme informs both the layout of the course and the art direction. For instance, the first level is titled Grim Furry Tales, a play on *Grimm's Fairy Tales*. The level takes place in a forest and underground cavern setting with common fairy tale elements such as Humpty Dumpty, Mother Goose, and the old woman who lives in a shoe. The themed art is scarce and one can assume that the Game Boy's technical limitations prevented more elaborate art design. The rest of the levels go on this way: Pirates of the Scratchibbean aboard a pirate ship, 9 1/2 Shrieks and its ghost-filled haunted house, or the Arabian-themed I Scream of Genie in which the Indian character Apu makes a poorly considered appearance. (One of many times that the character's heritage has been leveraged for cheap laughs.)[5]

Just hanging with my best bro.

Levels do become more challenging over time, introducing environmental hazards such as water traps, cannon balls, and radioactive acid drops, as well as trick doors and cannons that send the ball to unintended parts of the level. These hazards are most perilous for causing the player to waste more strokes on the ball's journey toward the hole, resulting in a lower score at the end of the game. It may feel stressful to navigate the levels with so much in the way, but the good part of the game's design is a complete absence of a time limit. Players are free to ignore the ball completely and explore the area, and in fact that's the best strategy for dealing with Itchy. The game takes on a twisted hunting mechanic if the player chooses to venture out into the level to find and eliminate all the instances of Itchy, which always spawn in the same places and don't return when Itchy is killed. This breaks the game down into two distinct phases of hunting and then golfing that may not be as fun as a chaotic game of mini golf with Itchy in the mix, but it's by far the best strategy for achieving the best score.

Scratch a bean.

It's really a bizarre entry in the *Simpsons* game oeuvre, both for its mash-up premise and the oddly successful take on miniature golf. At the very least, Beam Software didn't grab the lowest hanging fruit on the tree as the developer of the other Itchy & Scratchy games did. Beam Software reached a little higher and achieved a unique take on the cat vs. mouse formula, even if it wasn't an entirely mind-blowing marriage of genres. And anyway, I'm pretty sick of games starring Bart Simpson. At first he was cute and funny, but now he's just annoying.

Notes

1. Bob Mackey, Henry Gilbert, and Chris Antista, "Talking Simpsons Interviews Paul Provenzano," *Talking Simpsons* (Patreon, 2017). Retrieved 2 April 2018.

2. Aaron Demeter, "Lee Carvallo's Putting Challenge" (itch.io, 2020). Originally created for the 1995 episode of *The Simpsons*, "Marge Be Not Proud," directed by Steven Dean Moore and written by Mike Scully.

3. "Dead Putting Society," *The Simpsons* (Fox Television, 1990). Directed by Rich Moore and written by Jeff Martin.

4. "I Married Marge," *The Simpsons* (Fox Television, 1991). Directed by Jeffrey Lynch and written by Jeff Martin.

5. *The Problem With Apu* (truTV, 2017). Directed by Michael Melamedoff and written by Hari Kondabolu.

Chapter 12: The Grab Bag

Virtual Bart - October 1994

My personal lack of history with *Simpsons* games continued through the mid-nineties. I was twelve by 1994 and while still very much into *The Simpsons* television show and also into video games, I leaned toward more action-friendly franchises such as *Sonic* and *X-Men*. *The Simpsons* just didn't move me to buy their games. However, I have a distinct memory centered around *Virtual Bart* for Sega Genesis. The American concept of the shopping mall continued unabated during this period, with grand malls gracing the landscape every few miles in my native Los Angeles. Our local mall was the Fox Hills Mall in Culver City, California.

As kids, we roamed to our personal favorite stores such as Software Etc. (a precursor to GameStop) and the legendary K.B. Toys. That latter stalwart of malls across America was the toy store of choice for many a kid and every parent's worst nightmare around Christmas time. It was the K.B. Toys store in Fox Hills where I encountered a box for *Virtual Bart* on the Sega Genesis. I contemplated it briefly (the first time I'd considered spending my own allowance on a *Simpsons* game), but that's not why I remember this occasion. It stood out because this Sega

Genesis game was hanging in a section with a giant Nintendo sign hanging above it. It was a flagrant disregard for the unspoken rule of the (retroactively named) Console Wars.[1] You can like the Super Nintendo, and you can like the Sega Genesis, but never the twain shall meet. Even today, retail stores that stock video games make sure to separate each company's games into their own respective aisles. It was a strange and jarring sight but somehow appropriate for a *Simpsons* game to thumb its nose at video game society. But for all that anguish, I didn't feel compelled to buy the *Virtual Bart* game. It would still be some time before I'd take the leap.

The Simpsons predicted VR nausea.

Sculptured Software thrived like so many developers of the era on the strength of licensed games. After all, there was no Google or YouTube available to easily search for fun games to play, and no influencers beyond the marketing dollars of the game publishers and word-of-mouth on the playground. So more often than not, kids or their parents selected games at the store based on familiarity. Long established franchises like *Super Mario Bros.* and *Mega Man* were safe bets, but the power of familiar characters like Mickey Mouse, Bugs Bunny, and Bart Simpson were guaranteed to sell some games. Paul Provenzano, the former Acclaim producer interviewed by the team at *Talking Simpsons*, believes this was one of Acclaim's core strengths:

> Acclaim had this edge, in my opinion at the time, because one: they were dealing with licensed properties that people recognized, and two: they were dealing with people that had experience in marketing a lot of products and a lot of different things. They were pretty savvy, so you know, it was a good combination for that.[2]

Sculptured Software saw a banner year in 1994 with nearly a dozen of their games released in stores alongside *Virtual Bart*, their last *Simpsons* game. Their releases include licensed games such as *The Ren and Stimpy Show: Time Warp*, *The Punisher*, and *Looney Tunes B-Ball*. It would be the peak of their company's production. Acclaim swooped in to buy the studio in 1995 and quickly pivoted the

Utah-based company into a development house for hockey and wrestling games. Sculptured Software would eventually be renamed to Iguana West before being shuttered completely when Acclaim faced bankruptcy in the early aughts. It's an unfortunate but unsurprising conclusion. Many studios that succeeded on the backs of 8-bit and 16-bit platforms would struggle to find their footing at the dawn of the 3D era.

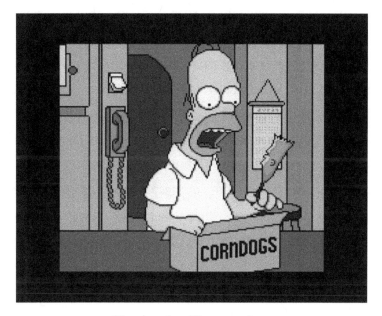

That's a familiar corn dog.

Game designers of the late eighties and nineties were faced with a peculiar challenge: make video games more difficult so that kids can't complete them in a single rental. It's a gauntlet thrown down in service of the company's bottom line, not unlike arcade game designers who tried to shake as many quarters as possible out of kids' pockets by making sure they died often in their games, forcing frequent pauses in gameplay when players died and needed to add another quarter. Home game designers similarly strived to draw out the experience so they could wring as many dollars out of customers' hands as possible, whether by cajoling them to rent a game more than once or just outright buy it.

That's one possibility that explains the surprising difficulty of *Virtual Bart*. The other possibility is the designers were short on content and couldn't have players get through it too easily lest they complain about the disparity between a short play time and high cost. I will get into specifics, but if we go by the numbers there are six levels in the game, with half of those levels consisting of only one or two stages a piece. The lean levels are generally the levels that introduce variations on third-person action in which Bart sits in the middle of the screen and dodges stuff, throws stuff, or some combination of the two. The latter levels are the side-scrolling platformer levels and they are the real doozy. Fortunately, the game includes a practice mode in which players may select any of the game's six levels and play them as many times as they like. The cutscenes are missing but it allows players to develop the skills necessary to complete the game's story mode.

Gameplay begins after short introductory cutscenes lay out the premise teased by the game's title. Bart attends the Springfield Elementary school science fair and gets snared into becoming a test subject in a virtual reality experiment. The final shot of Bart wearing virtual reality goggles and strapped to the machine then segues into the level selection menu. Unlike the intricate hub world introduced in *Bart's Nightmare*, *Virtual Bart* merely employs a game of wheel of fortune as Bart spins around in the center of the screen, waiting for the player to press a button and make a selection. Bart's momentum forces him to rotate a bit longer after a button is pressed and he stops on one of the six levels in the menu. There is also the seventh bonus slot that introduces the risk versus reward aspect of the selection menu. The top slot fluctuates between images of a corn dog that grants an extra life and a skull that takes away a life. And indeed, while each level has a limited set of lives, so does the level selection menu. Players can eventually figure out the timing of Bart's rotations to land on the exact level they want or even nail that elusive corn dog, but the game only allows the player to earn so many corn dogs before limiting the bonus slot to only display the skull. Can't reward skilled players too much, eh?

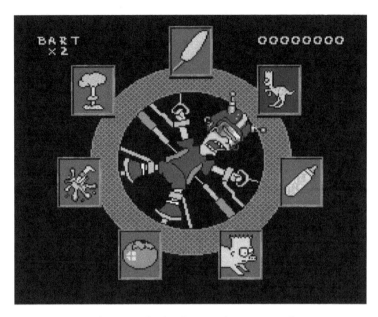

He has no choice but to choose poorly.

The captive Bart rotates clockwise, so let's follow along. The first level after the bonus slot is the Dino Bart level. This first platformer level is also the game's longest and most traditional. The gameplay features a long-necked Bart-osaurus hopping and tail-whipping his way across a prehistoric landscape crawling with dinosaurs and de-evolved takes on various Springfieldians, including an impressive array of voice clips for them. The environments vary from outdoor mountainsides to caverns and then an icy river, but the general feel of the level is that of scaling a mountain to get to the top. There are no puzzles to solve and the only real obstacles are the jumps and enemies that must be

170

overcome to proceed. None of the enemies are especially difficult to defeat but the level is designed to inflict death by a thousand paper cuts.

Everything wants to attack Bart. The game design certainly encourages avoiding enemies where possible and turns the whole thing into a funny sort of survival horror experience. Enemies are oftentimes placed right on the player's path, forcing a confrontation that ends with at least a few slivers of health whacked away by an enemy dinosaur or a caveman's rock. Bart's tail whip attack has some extra reach that helps with avoiding enemy attacks, but they're all jacked up on caveman speed or something because they are *very* aggressive. And then some enemies (like Lisa with a bow and arrow or Krusty juggling skulls) will just chip away health at a distance. The game does grant Bart extra health in the form of what I can only guess is the game designer's favorite food: corn dogs. Occasionally, power-ups that grant Bart the ability to roar can be used to clear the screen of enemies. The journey to the top of the mountain and across the glacier ends with an encounter with Moe and Homer atop sheets of ice. It's a dull twist where the player can't attack them directly but must instead whip away the ice sheets until they are at the same level as the player. One final whip causes them both to, um, explode, and the player's reward is a short cutscene showing prehistoric Homer's icy fate.

The next level in line is perhaps the most difficult: Baby Bart. While technically a platformer level, the design is focused on showing off Baby Bart's gymnastic ability. And unlike the Dino Bart level, this one is actually based on a scene from the show. In the fourth season episode titled "Lisa's First Word," Marge and Homer recount their days as a young married couple raising Baby Bart. A montage of scenes ensues in which Bart causes mischief, including the scene where a bare-cheeked Bart swings around on a clothesline. This extraordinary swinging ability becomes the core mechanic for the level. The first stage is a wooded area behind the Simpson house in which the player must guide Baby Bart along a series of branches by jumping and latching onto them. There are a few platforms for Bart to balance upon but not many. Mundane enemies such as squirrels and birds also appear to mix up the obstacles until players eventually reach a clothesline. Unlike the television episode or that tree stage, Bart simply has to balance on the clothesline tracks and dodge clothing or animals that would cause him to fall. Bart isn't completely helpless as he faces these obstacles; he is granted the ability to fire off pacifiers like he's packing a machine gun.

This leads to a wild aerial chase with Bart hitching a ride on a balloon, but the gameplay is similar—dodge the obstacles and shoot pacifiers at anything that moves. The dodging continues in the stroller race against baby versions of the bullies Jimbo and Kearney, then leads into a ball-balancing act where Baby Bart can only bounce on balls balancing on seals' noses. The final act is a trek across a circus tent full of swinging trapeze and bouncy trampolines. This stage takes all the previously utilized designs and combines them into a hellish gauntlet of swinging, jumping, and terrifying clowns. It seems like more trouble than it's worth for some ice cream, but what do I know? Maybe babies know the real score.

Is iguana kosher?

The third and final platforming level is by far the most horrifying: Pig Bart. It features Bart transmogrified into pig form and stuck in a Krusty-branded pork factory with clowns as factory workers and corporate big wigs as the final bosses. Fans will recall that Krusty had a heart attack while hocking his pork wares on television, and as a Jewish character has a complicated relationship to pork.[3]

But he's also a dedicated capitalist, so here we see the natural next step in his commercial efforts.

Pig Bart's goal is to free his compatriots from the shackles of their imprisonment using only a few abilities. He can jump as is the way in a platformer, but the player can also perform a bounce jump not unlike Scrooge McDuck's pogo cane in the *DuckTales* games on NES. Bart must use this ability often as he traverses the terrors of a pork factory. The whole concept is like a cartoon take on *The Jungle*, an early twentieth century novel which highlighted the horrors of the meatpacking industry.[4] Each stage of the level features pigs being frozen, cooked, and processed into Krusty-branded cans of ham. The player can also face a gruesome end if they accidentally fall into one of the machines, leaving behind a yellow can of ham with Pig Bart's visage on the side. The stages all illustrate a step in the pork production process, starting with the canning room. This first area is full of conveyor belts and funnels leading to large machines. Pigs go in, canned ham comes out.

The clown factory workers serve more as guards, patrolling the halls and ready to attack Pig Bart if he crosses their path. This area also includes a novel idea: puzzles! They take the form of locked doors that can only be opened with a key that matches the color on the lock. It's a bit frustrating to have to hunt down these locked doors when there is no explanation of the task required, but it's a welcome addition in a game where most of the platforming is rote and straightforward. Navigating the canning room leads to the freezer, where pigs frozen in blocks of ice are carried off to meet their grisly fate. The final disturbing set piece is a journey through the broiler area—a collection of fire traps, receding platforms, and hydraulic presses that are all designed to chip away at the precious little health available to the player. The final room is the pork factory's conference room where a group of Three Stooges-like corporate suits do their best to wallop Pig Bart into mashed ham. Defeating the bosses leads to the final release of Bart's pig buddies and a cheerful end to their story... until you remember that millions of other pigs are still on the chopping block.

Bart was always going to throw the tomato.

And that's just the first half of the game. But things move along much more quickly after those meaty platform levels, which may be a good thing if the player has endured the game thus far. The next level is the class picture session. Bart sits in the foreground and then leaves it to the player to toss the limited bushel of tomatoes (and eggs in stage two) toward the kids walking across the school grounds. The gameplay is similar to golf mechanics in other video games. Press the button to charge a throw, then press the button again to toss at that point. Players can also press Left or Right on the D-pad to angle the throw to the sides.

And you may need to go for those sharp angles—the first stage sees the kids simply walk horizontally from one side of the screen to the other. Hitting one of the kids removes them from the crowd, whereas allowing them to pass unsplattered will cause them to reappear at a different distance each time. But of course it can't be that easy, so a squad of adults also march back and forth between the kids. Hitting an adult is an instant game over for the level, so it's essential to watch one's aim. However, Principal Skinner will occasionally bend over to tie his shoelaces, giving you a prime bonus target. This may remind you of a certain scene where Lisa makes the mistake of asking Bart to hold her science fair tomato for a moment.[5] This tomato frenzy leads to the egg barrage on the playground of stage two. The gameplay is identical, but the kids now move in and out of the background, creating a more chaotic space in which perfectly aligned shots can miss as the kids move closer or further away. Well, there's always that practice mode.

Speaking of practice, a player may find themselves so lost in this next level that they'll need plenty of it. Mount Splashmore is a seemingly simple journey down a plastic tube full of water, but it turns out to be a hellish maze full of sharks, dogs, three-eyed fish, submarines, blubber butts, and way too many kids. This water slide consists of a series of forks in the path that must be navigated in order to survive to the end. Some wrong ways only end with a face full of Homer's butt or an inexplicably non-lethal fall into a lion's mouth, but other paths lead to certain death off the edge of a cliff or face-first into a sign. All is not hopeless though, and several items can help the player survive. Clocks add extra seconds to the stage timer, the ever-present corn dogs give extra health, and boogie boards can be used as temporary invincibility against the obstacles. A few differences occur depending on whether it's the SNES or Sega Genesis version. For example, Genesis players can use the C-button to duck under the water or grab and throw beach balls to fend off other sliders, but SNES players don't have the option. Conversely, SNES players have a helpful arrow flash at the beginning to tell them which fork in the path to follow, but Sega Genesis players only have the option to stare at the back of a fat, bald man to see some vague arrows pointing the way. Or, you know, just hug the bald man tight and follow him. They're strange design choices, and the fact that the Sega Genesis version released months later indicates that the designers may have decided they'd made it too easy on SNES. Ultimately, the correct path leads to... a swimming pool. It may be anti-climactic, but perhaps the game designers take their water slide narratives seriously.

I'm just going to drive my bike like this, and if you get flattened, it's your own fault.

We follow that cheerful day at the water park with a delightful jaunt on the highways of post-apocalyptic Springfield. The Doomsday Bart level features a leather-and spike-clad Bart doing his best impression of the *Road Warrior*, riding his motorcycle along abandoned highways toward the ruins of the city. Much like Mount Splashmore, this level is a tough survival to the end of the line. Gameplay for the level is liberally borrowed from that motorcycle combat classic, *Road Rash*. And just like those helmeted street riders, Bart can kick to the sides to knock the street bullies out of the way. He is also equipped with a water balloon gun to fire ahead as the bullies appear in front of him. The street bullies actively try to take out Bart, but Otto and his bus also appear from time to time to cause massive damage. But no post-apocalypse can be complete without rubble and critters littering the road, creating even more obstacles on Bart's journey to the end. Players who dodge all these obstacles are rewarded with the best ending in the game: an original couch gag in which Bart enters the ruins of the Simpson house and joins the skeletons of his family on the couch, scattering their bones in the process. Bart stares at the tube and sees what can only be the image of Krusty in his head, whose imaginary voice yells out "Hey, surviving kids!", his cackles echoing through the emptiness.

Frankenstein had to start somewhere.

That's as apt a note as any to end the game. The final cutscene shows Bart finally free himself from the virtual simulation only for Homer to step into it, laughing and crying as he twirls and twirls away into the distance, leaving players with the same dizzying sense of emptiness. It's a strange game that arrived at a strange time in the game industry, marking the end of players' interest in the virtual life of Bart Simpson but only whetting Fox's appetite for selling *Simpsons* games to unsuspecting fans.

Notes

1. Blake J. Harris, *Console Wars: Sega, Nintendo, and the Battle That Defined a Generation* (New York: HarperCollins, 2014).

2. Bob Mackey, Henry Gilbert, and Chris Antista, "Talking Simpsons Interviews Paul Provenzano," *Talking Simpsons* (Patreon, 2017). Retrieved 2 April 2018.

3. "Krusty Gets Busted," *The Simpsons* (Fox Television, 1990). Directed by Brad Bird and written by Jay Kogen and Wallace Wolodarsky.

4. Upton Sinclair, *The Jungle* (New York: Doubleday, Page & Co., 1906).

5. "Duffless," *The Simpsons* (Fox Television, 1993). Directed by Jim Reardon and written by David M. Stern.

Chapter 13: The Last Tango

The Itchy & Scratchy Game - February 1995

As a kid in the eighties and nineties, I was there for the tail end of comedic animated violence in its full glory. There were countless television shows that repackaged old cartoons from Warner Brothers, Disney, and Hanna-Barbera, among other studios, to fill half-hour slots on television stations that needed to pad out their daily programming blocks. This is how I usually caught what used to be short animated films that played before theatrical releases. I learned how Mickey Mouse used to be a mischievous fiend before he was watered down and turned into a corporate mascot, and that Warner Brothers shorts are rife with gun-totlin', anvil-droppin', quip-spewin' characters who routinely gave each other black eyes and concussions that disappeared in the next scene. I also learned how casual racism and sexism were thrown in alongside the casual violence, making rewatches of these so-called "classic" cartoons a hard pill to swallow.

But there's one pair of characters from the era who are especially relevant to this chapter's game. They were titans of cartoon violence, appearing in over one hundred sixty animated shorts across nearly four decades. These mute animal protagonists were caught in an eternal chase where a cat hunts a mouse and always comes close to catching him, but is ultimately outwitted at every turn. I write, of course, of Tom and Jerry. Their film shorts were created and developed by Hanna-Barbera, and distributed by MGM for decades. Eventually, the merger parade caught up and threw all of Hanna-Barbera's works under the Warner Brothers umbrella, and now Tom and Jerry live alongside their once-competitor characters such as Sylvester the Cat and Tweety Bird. The old Tom and Jerry shorts are available online at the Internet Archive, and while the violence in their initial cartoons isn't too horrifying, their means of maiming each other gets worse over the course of the series.[1] There's also the aforementioned casual racism in the form of the Mammy caricature who routinely appears to scold Tom for his messes.[2] The cartoons can still be enjoyed, even with an eye on the problematic nature of old media.

Oh no.

Like me, many of the creators on *The Simpsons* grew up watching Tom and Jerry on their tiny tube televisions. All of the writers in the early days of the show came from traditional live action sitcoms or talk shows, and they slowly learned that they could get quite a lot wackier in an animated medium. The Simpsons themselves were often embroiled in violence, though it was usually Homer getting into a ridiculous fight or Bart getting beat up by bullies. But the writers seemingly wanted to take it to the extreme without breaking the reality of the show ("Treehouse of Horror" episodes notwithstanding). And so they created their altered reality: "The Itchy & Scratchy Show." Itchy was the stand-in for Jerry the mouse, and

Scratchy the counterpart to Tom's wily cat in pursuit. They shared the same dynamic wherein Scratchy is always trying to catch Itchy, but while Tom and Jerry engaged in light-hearted torture, Itchy & Scratchy outright tried to murder one another, with Itchy usually succeeding with one macabre plan or another. It was not uncommon for Scratchy to be maimed, melted, torn apart, or have internal organs viciously removed. Bart and Lisa love it when they watch this, of course. The cartoon violence is dealt with head-on in the second season episode, "Itchy & Scratchy & Marge." Marge tries and briefly succeeds at getting cartoon creators to ban violence on the show for the sake of the children, but this is ultimately overturned when Marge is unable to justify censoring one artistic medium while sparing another.

While television writers wrestled with the ethics of cartoon violence, countless children played countless violent video games on their home consoles, and I was among them. Really, Itchy & Scratchy and their progenitors were quite tame by comparison.

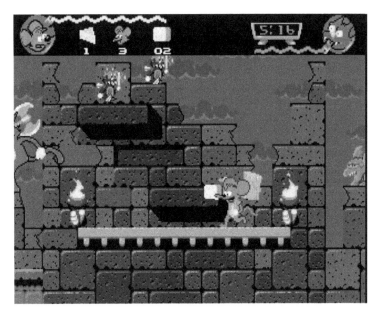

Chasin' down the babies.

Itchy & Scratchy translated to video game antagonists quite easily, first showing up as enemies with their own themed level in *Bart's House of Weirdness* (Chapter 5) and then again in *Bart's Nightmare* (Chapter 7). Someone at Acclaim then decided they were interesting enough to star in their own games, making their first headline appearance in *Itchy & Scratchy in Miniature Golf Madness* on Game Boy. As detailed in Chapter 11, that game featured Scratchy as the protagonist who kills Itchy many times in the game, an odd reversal considering Itchy is always the one who kills Scratchy on the television show. That's where *The Itchy & Scratchy Game* comes in. With Itchy as the star, players could finally unleash the kind of cartoon mayhem they'd been watching on *The Simpsons* for over five years.

Acclaim needed a studio to develop this new Itchy & Scratchy title, and for one reason or another (likely the bottom line) they turned away from their previous collaborators. They wound up making the deal with Bits Corporation (later known as Bits Studios), a game developer based in London. They'd only just started in 1990, but like other studios in this book, their focus was almost entirely on ports and licensed games. They took a stab at licensed fare such as *Spider-Man*, *Terminator*, and oddballs like a game based on the 1994 version of *Mary Shelley's Frankenstein*. And like the other companies, they fared a lot better in the days of 8- and 16-bit games, with seventy-five percent of their catalogue released before the dawn of the 3D era with the PlayStation's debut in 1995. Bits Corporation continued to release games for about another decade until the studio was dissolved by their parent company, leaving no trace as their assets and properties were liquidated into obscurity.

Duel of the fates.

Itchy & Scratchy have no lore to speak of, like those previously cited cartoon inspirations. They are merely vessels of the age-old relationship between predator and prey. But of course in this case, the mouse is the vastly superior predator, relentlessly catching and mutilating his cat prey. And this is what the video game presents for players: play as Itchy, and kill Scratchy... a whole lot. That's all. I understand some players don't quibble over narrative, but this player always appreciates any thought put toward the underlying story as a character is guided along from one side of the screen to the other. *The Itchy & Scratchy Game* just presents a series of levels and enemies with no particular motive beyond cartoon murder, which I suppose is appropriate for the characters but does put into question the choice to turn "The Itchy & Scratchy Show" into a video game in the first place.

The game plays out in a repeated cycle of two stages: first, Itchy must fight through a platforming area full of Scratchy and his myriad weapons, environmental hazards, and small wind-up copies of Scratchy that hunt down Itchy like an army of possessed demon dolls. They're easy to kill but are just a constant annoyance, always appearing on whatever platform Itchy is standing. Itchy can find a dizzying array of gruesome weapons scattered throughout the stages, in addition to power-ups like extra lives, cheesy speed boosts, health kits, and temporary invincibility. The mini-Scratchys also provide the ammunition for Itchy's ranged weapons in the level, all of which vary but are identical in their function. They're simply objects to throw at Scratchy, although they're not really necessary until the second stage. In fact, the primary strategy of the first stage is to hoard the ammunition so Itchy is better prepared for the boss fight in the second stage. I guess the player is also supposed to kill Scratchy until his health bar is at zero, but it's an easy and unexceptional task to complete.

The real challenge in the game—besides suffering Scratchy's horrible shriek of pain—is the boss fights. They begin fairly easily, but with each successive level the boss fights become more and more challenging, introducing elaborate contraptions and hazards that Itchy must avoid while trying to toss weapons at Scratchy's vehicle. But the challenge comes entirely from the level design. The strategy is always the same: hang back and lob objects at Scratchy. The only difference is the level of dodging the player has to perform in between those lobs.

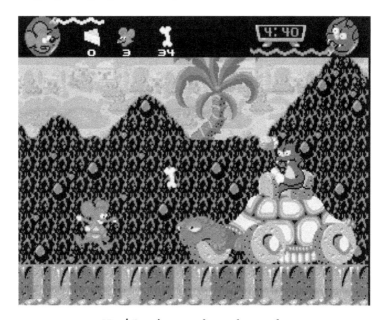

Hey! Don't scratch up the turtle.

So it's safe to say that the gameplay wasn't exceptional. There isn't even an ending scene or text to congratulate the player. It all just ends with a credit roll. This makes sense; each level of the game is presented with a title card as if it's a self-contained episode of "The Itchy & Scratchy Show." However, when each level is just the exact same gameplay with a change of scenery, well, it kind of dulls the impact. But that touches on the areas where the game succeeds, namely the art and theming of each level. Although the animations and backgrounds are kind of bland and stiff, they're also big and accurate, a feature that is noteworthy in contrast with previous *Simpsons* games on home systems. The series thus far has generally been bad at actually capturing the art design from the show. This game is arguably the first outside of *The Simpsons* arcade game to really nail down the look of the animated characters. The backgrounds and enemy characters are also well-animated and bright, although the environments give the vibe of props on a stage instead of real aspects of the environment. Each of the seven levels has a typical video game level theme, ranging from the prehistoric "Juracid Bath" to the mechanized "Disassembly Line." But this is what players have to look forward to if they attempt to complete the game—it looks good. That's... something.

Given how brief and simple the game is, one has to wonder if it's as they originally intended. I can see it now: Acclaim is shipping licensed games left and right, but these are licenses they've been peddling in the video game space for years. Each game gets a little more expensive and a little less lucrative. And with *The Simpsons*, it was clear they'd started cutting costs since the last couple of Game Boy games and *Virtual Bart* on consoles, where the developers clearly went lean on the amount of content they squeezed into the games. Furthermore, the good folks at The Cutting Room Floor—a web catalog of the hidden content and debug features in video games—revealed that the SNES version of the game actually contains dialogue text from Bart, Lisa, and Krusty the clown, indicating that the game was originally designed to include framing cutscenes where Krusty introduces the levels and Bart and Lisa comment on them as if they're watching episodes of the show. This dialogue isn't stellar, including lines such as "Woo Woo Woo!!! This is the one when Itchy is a red Indian," so these may only be leftover bits from ideas that were tested early in the design process and abandoned. But really, it's unlikely that these (sometimes offensive) scenes would have helped improve the gameplay.[3]

Itchy's cartoon invincibility is no more.

There are other signs that *The Itchy & Scratchy Game* wasn't quite all it could have been. For one, the version for the Sega Genesis that went as far as being reviewed in game magazines like GamePro didn't actually make it to store shelves.[4] It's not clear if it even made it to the factory, but it's likely that pre-release copies were shipped to reviewers before Acclaim decided it wasn't worth the expense to distribute a Sega Genesis version in early 1995. It must have been one of these review copies that allowed savvy web pirates to create and distribute a ROM for players to play to this day. But Sega players did get an official release of the game, just on a much tinier screen. The Sega Game Gear game shipped alongside the SNES version, presenting a crunched down take on the game that strips away the game's one positive quality: its art. The Game Gear characters are smaller by necessity but suffer for it, looking like the characters were thrown into a hydraulic press and squished down to fit. It's cute in a way. But I'll tell you what's not cute—the game has no boss fights. You know, the one challenging aspect of the console games? Yeah, not here at all. The player's only objective is to hunt down and kill Scratchy in each of the levels and move along until it ends. Also, the underwater high-jinks of level 4's "The Pusseidon Adventure" are no more; the level was cut. So tinier sprites, no bosses, and one less level... it's a tough sell.

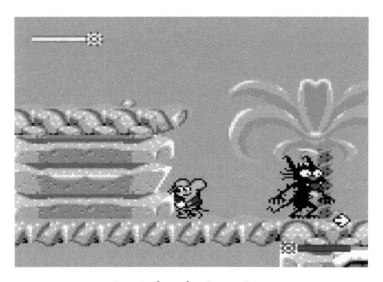

Roasted on the Game Gear.

The Itchy & Scratchy Game is a notable last game in several categories: the last 16-bit *Simpsons* game, the last *Simpsons* game from both Acclaim and Bits Corporation (which only worked on this one), and really the last game from that intense early period of *The Simpsons*. Season six of the show was in full swing, showcasing episodes from the peak of the classic era. Legendary episodes like "A Star Is Burns" and "Lisa's Wedding" premiered around the launch of this game into stores, during a time when the show was at its wackiest but the merchandise had begun to die down. There is no clearer sign than the fact that the world went on without a new *Simpsons* video game until 1997, and even then the game was only released for Windows and Macintosh computers, leaving console players out in the cold for six years. Of course, given the reception to the dubious quality of *Simpsons* games from the early nineties, it might have been a relief.

Notes

1. "Tom & Jerry All Episodes (389)" (Internet Archive, 2018). Archived on archive.org. Retrieved 20 March 2021.
2. Lizzie Crocker, "Is 'Tom and Jerry' Really Racist?" (The Daily Beast, 2014). Retrieved 20 March 2021.
3. "The Itchy & Scratchy Game (SNES)" (The Cutting Room Floor, 2021). Retrieved 20 March 2021.
4. "GamePro Issue 68" (GamePro, 1995). Archived by Sketch the Cow on archive.org. Retrieved 20 March 2021.

Chapter 14: The Virtual Voyeur

Virtual Springfield - August 1997

Oh, jeez, we're up to 1997. I have to think back. Where was I? A fifteen-year-old, just starting high school, and not into the old *Simpsons* games at all. I was perhaps playing *Resident Evil* and *Tomb Raider* on the PlayStation, trying my best to play the mature stuff. That said, I was absolutely still watching *The Simpsons* on broadcast television. That's the year when Bill Oakley and Josh Weinstein ended their time as showrunners and Mike Scully came aboard to run the ship. That's also when I took the leap into recording episodes.

I have vivid memories of my first forays into VHS dubbing, with multiple old eighties VCRs tethered together as I transferred episodes of *The Simpsons* with the commercials crudely edited out. I ended up with two tapes—one for general favorite episodes, and another specifically for the "Treehouse of Horror" specials. These tapes even followed me to work where I kept them to watch on the small TV-VCR that we kept in the store room for new employee training videos. I'm convinced I got a few coworkers into the show by virtue of that being the only entertainment in the back room during lunch breaks. Incidentally, season nine premiered in 1997 with "The

City of New York vs. Homer Simpson," the coincidental first entry on my VHS tape of favorite episodes.

I have to think that if the Simpsons were still starring in video games during those years when I finally had some disposable income, I would have been all-in. But it was a silent time. Nothing new on SNES, Sega Genesis, Sega Saturn, Sony PlayStation, or Nintendo 64. This dearth of interactive *Simpsons* merch coincided with the tech world's focus on the exciting possibilities of multimedia. The times they were a-changin', and Fox would not get left behind.

The limitless possibilities of multimedia CD-ROMs.

So, sure, I was nerding it up with the best of them with my *Simpsons* tapes and PlayStation, but there was a notable hole in my life—no computer! My family took their sweet time in adding one of those seemingly benign beige boxes to our household, and in truth I wasn't clamoring for one. The Internet was still in its nascent stages, and only the most knowledgeable or curious cared about using Prodigy or AOL to go "on-line" and discover the wonders of bulletin boards and crudely designed web content. But a few companies were catching on, including our old friends at Fox. Their web presence dates back to at least 1996 when they began putting up product websites for their film, television, and yes, even video game properties. Fox also made a crucial decision in the years since the SNES and Sega Genesis ruled: they would become their own developer and publisher of video games. They formed a new division called Fox Interactive to oversee and produce all video games and interactive media that leveraged their properties. There were no more middle managers like Acclaim using subcontractors to put out subpar products. Fox would take on the responsibility—and the financial risk—to release the games themselves. According to producer Paul Provenzano, who jumped ship from Acclaim to Fox, it all came from just where one would expect:

> Fox Interactive was concept pitched by the licensing person who was in charge of video games. It was a guy named Scott Marcus, and he was always the guy that used to show up out of the blue and say "No" to everything... So Scott had

looked around at all the games, that mostly Acclaim were doing with Fox properties, and he knew who the developers were. So he pitched to his boss, who took him directly to [Fox CEO] Murdoch, and said, "We should be doing these games." And it worked![1]

And this may explain their approach with their first release since 1995's *The Itchy & Scratchy Game*. With the previous publisher deals terminated, Fox had to start from scratch. That means hiring project managers, programmers, artists, animators, and other support staff that are required to make and ship video games. I'm sure the time needed to build that team is part of the reason for the two-year delay since the last game. But beyond that, Fox Interactive needed to build relationships with entities like Nintendo, Sony, and Sega, all of which were part of the deal when signing with existing publishers. I can't say for sure, of course, but I'd guess all of these factors weighed in on the platforms Fox would target for their first game releases. While they did ship a few games on consoles before 1997—such as *The Tick* and *Die Hard Trilogy*—they were primarily the publisher and other companies took on development duties.

Having a bit of a meltdown.

Fox Interactive had already dipped their toes into multimedia PC releases with a cartoon-maker application called *The Simpsons Cartoon Studio* from 1996, which featured a tool that allowed PC users to create and export their own small *Simpsons* cartoons with officially licensed art, animation, and sounds. They followed that with *Virtual Springfield*, released exclusively for Windows and Macintosh computers in 1997, with Fox Interactive as the publisher and companies called Vortex Media Arts and Digital Evolution taking on developer duties. The dual developer situation arose when Vortex Media Arts, as the original developer, went out of business. According to PC Gamer's interview with Michael Viner, lead designer on the project, Digital Evolution swooped in to finish the work. Recalls Viner:

> But Digital Evolution bought the contract for *Virtual Springfield*. Around that time, it was like the dot com boom and everybody was everything. They had a lot of projects. They were very legitimate; but they didn't have a gaming division.[2]

It's worth noting that this was Digital Evolution's one video game credit, which is not surprising when most of the company is working on car brand websites and slot machines. And it wasn't just Fox Interactive heading up the project. This was also the first project in which Gracie Films—which produces the television show—was heavily involved, helping the development team with dialogue, wrangling voice actors, creative direction, and all the involvement that we would have liked to see since the beginning. And hell, it really shows. *Virtual Springfield* is an impressive game, heavy on the gags and jokes that any *Simpsons* fan would have loved to see. The actual game aspect is fairly light, with no real objective beyond exploration, but it is robust enough that I have no qualms about including it here as a game worth discussing alongside the others in the book.

This was also a time when certain names kept appearing in the credits, and I've since come to see these people as the caretakers of the *Simpsons* license during that tumultuous dot-com era. People like Mike Schneider, Luke Letizia, and Harish Rao, all of whom carried on as producers and directors of every *Simpsons* game developed during the era. Christopher Tyng is also a notable addition to the credits list, appearing as composer for a bunch of *Simpsons* video games in addition to his contributions as composer for *Futurama* and many other television shows. Provenzano credits two individuals with really making the effort to ensure it was an outstanding *Simpsons* experience:

> That was through the effort of both the project producer, Gary Sheinwald—who was a devoted Simpsons fan—and the associate producer, Luke Letizia, who was meticulous to a fault. He was the guy that went through and pulled hundreds and hundreds of possible Easter eggs from the show that we could include. That was a labor of love for both of them because they just loved *The Simpsons* so much.[3]

It's officially the beginning of the Fox Interactive era, and let me tell you, it's going to be a real roller coaster.

Ah yes, another one of Springfield's beloved regulars.

You know, it's funny to find out that the staff at *The Simpsons* didn't really have a series bible in those early days. A series bible is a collection of guides on the characters and their relationships, locations in the show, the characters' design, and so forth. But they had no time for that. They just kind of made up characters and locations as they needed them, episode-by-episode. It sounds crazy, but in their own wacky way the teams at Gracie Films and Fox were building a world without limits, where the Nuclear Power Plant could be on the edge of Springfield in one episode and in the Simpsons' backyard in another. This made for a more versatile development process for the television show and a nightmare for anyone who needed to build this space for a video game. None of the previous game teams needed to worry about this because, well, it doesn't matter where everyone and everything is located when you can just transport the player from level to level like some kinda digital magic.

But that wasn't the kind of game that the team at Fox Interactive wanted to make. They'd seen enough weird platformers with little connection to the show beyond characters resembling their television counterparts and a few sound bites. They were going to go for the gusto: recreate all of Springfield as an interactive, fully explorable world. Provenzano remembers a very clear creative direction:

> So our focus was to let people live in that world, and along the way you needed some kind of gameplay. That also meant you had to meet all these characters, and we needed people to write a lot of these characters' lines.[4]

For the first time, players could move about in the town of Springfield, free to check out the Mayor's office at Town Hall, the Nuclear Power Plant (which is back on the outskirts of town), and of course, 742 Evergreen Terrace. They decided the player would be an interactive observer in the world, not unlike Lisa when she imagines a world where virtual reality would allow her to explore the world of Gengis Khan in the season four episode, "Marge Vs. The Monorail." The good people at Fox Interactive wanted us to go where the Simpsons go, defile who they defile, and eat who they eat.

Rude dude with an attitude.

That's where the adventure begins. As the player, we are equipped with a virtual reality visor that transports us to the center of Springfield, where Troy McClure (voiced by Phil Hartman a year before his untimely death) introduces the player to the world of Springfield and to the first clear use of the interactive medium with one of several custom introductions, randomly selected when the game is loaded. After the introduction, the player is left in the town center with little direction and several menu options as part of the "Really Virtual Viewthingy" display, including an inventory for collected items and a town map of Springfield. According to the PC Gamer article and Provenzano's interview with *Talking Simpsons*, it was quite the effort to map out an explorable Springfield when the show's creators made no such attempt. As Viner recalls for PC Gamer:

> They admittedly paid no attention to [continuity] when they were making *The Simpsons*... If they needed something for an episode, they just created it. And they didn't think much about how it hooked into a neighbourhood. That was a big challenge for us—figuring out where things were located in juxtaposition in creating a map for Springfield.[5]

The entire game takes place from a first-person perspective and instantly reminds one of *Myst* and its many clones and imitators that proliferated in the wake of that game's success in the early nineties. *Virtual Springfield* is essentially a point-and-click adventure game with elaborate animated transitions from one scene to the next. The player can use the mouse and interactive arrows to move around along prescribed routes, and every once in a while they'll run into a location they can explore. The gameplay may stretch thin over time, but to a fresh player in 1997 it must have been a wonder to have some measure of freedom in exploring the town.

They said hang a left at the star.

For instance, walking along Evergreen Terrace can lead to Ned Flanders's house, and clicking on the house leads to the rumpus room in the basement where Ned and his family pop up for random quips and gags. Players can also dig into their personal belongings and poke objects to get a close-up view of things like an Emergency Baptism Kit or The Big Book of Religious Answers, which answers questions like "Does the devil read Cosmo?" Further investigation of the rumpus room leads to another of the game's interactive showcases: mini games.

Oh boy, if you like mini games, *Virtual Springfield* has got you covered. The mini game in Ned's rumpus room requires shaking and squirting a bottle of seltzer at a variety of objects lined up on the shelves above Ned's bar. The mini game is the equivalent of a shooting gallery, and the prize is a series of gags that take place as water is squirted onto each object. There's a neat *Doom* parody at the Kwik-E-Mart called "Apoom" in which players fight off bullies with a broom and they, um, explode. Other mini games are contextual, such as the "Larry the Looter" arcade game at Noiseland Arcade. And this is what the game as a whole is like: walk along the street, enter a locale, and mess around with the stuff inside to find gags and scenes with the characters. This backfires a bit when players are traversing the town on the streets. While characters regularly pop up at intersections with a short scene or bit of dialogue, it can still feel like a ghost town. Later video game renditions of Springfield would ensure that there were plenty of townspeople wandering about uttering their signature quips, but it was difficult to pull off with the technical limitations of 1997.

There are two meatier aspects of the game's progression. For one, some gags and items are hidden behind puzzles that require players to find keys or other objects to unlock rooms for exploration. One of the more complex puzzle chains involves finding a note about gerbil food in Lisa's drawer at the Simpson house, then using that to find gerbil food in Miss Hoover's drawer at Springfield Elementary, and finally using that to open a cabinet beneath the gerbil cage in the classroom. A simpler example is taking a Krusty key from the Mayor's office and using it to get into Krustylu Studios.

There are also community cards hidden around the town's seventeen locations. They continue to randomly appear in the same limited set of locations and finding all seventy-four leads to a secret seventy-fifth card that shares a secret website link to more game-related secrets on the Internet. The website is longer active, of course, and seems to have contained extra bits of information about the game. You know Fox Interactive was serious about the Internet when they were sticking website addresses into their games.

Hiring for Danish pastry temp, payment in exposure.

The game plays slowly from our modern point of view, but the production value still shines. Fox Interactive did not skimp on ensuring that *Virtual Springfield* looked amazing, from the hand-drawn animations to the streets and environments that were clearly rendered in 3D but painted over so that the art style matched the traditional animation. All of the easter eggs and gags are lovingly rendered, showing that the developers wanted to display the same level of detail as the writers and designers of the television show. They matched this technical and artistic dedication with special attention to the writing and dialogue.

I've harped on the fact that previous games based on *The Simpsons* had little in the way of, you know, jokes. And while not every line in *Virtual Springfield* is a hum dinger on par with writing from the show, they do well with the jokes they implemented and have plenty of fun character moments. Even the actors took the opportunity to really go above and beyond. Provenzano recalls, "But then we went into the studio with the scripts and you get a couple of the actors, they were having fun with it! They just kept saying stuff, and they just kept adding more."[6] They even built an entire house as part of the promotions for this game.[7] Above all, it makes it feel like the player is *in* Springfield, with all its visual and comedic appeal and the dollars to back it up.

Grampa joined his local DSA chapter.

That's really the finest point I can put on this: *Virtual Springfield* was the first video game to capture the charm of *The Simpsons* in a video game. It's not an action-packed adventure, but developers had tried to make *The Simpsons* into an action game series for years with little success at achieving what the show did every week. This game introduced players to the possibility that if their *Simpsons* games couldn't reach the same heights as the television show, they could at least aim for something greater than run-of-the-mill gameplay with *Simpsons* characters slapped onto it. Recent ventures such as *The Simpsons Ride* (2008) and the "Planet of the Couches" VR couch gag on Google Cardboard (2016) demonstrate that there's still an appetite for *The Simpsons* in non-traditional types of interactive games.

Notes

1. Bob Mackey, Henry Gilbert, and Chris Antista, "Talking Simpsons Interviews Paul Provenzano," *Talking Simpsons* (Patreon, 2017). Retrieved 2 April 2018.
2. Jack Yarwood, "The story of Virtual Springfield, the Simpsons walking simulator that spawned a tourist attraction" (PC Gamer, 2020). Retrieved 20 March 2021.
3. Bob Mackey, Henry Gilbert, and Chris Antista.
4. Ibid.
5. Jack Yarwood.
6. Bob Mackey, Henry Gilbert, and Chris Antista.
7. Wendy Jackson, "Springfield, Nevada" (Animation World Magazine, 1997). Archived on awn.com. Retrieved 20 March 2021.

Chapter 15: The Two Strikes and a Turkey

The Simpsons Bowling - June 2000

Video arcade parlors had transformed since the heady days of *Pac-Man* and *Donkey Kong*. The technology evolved in leaps and bounds throughout the eighties, creating unique experiences and gameplay that could not be matched on home consoles. I looked at some of this history in writing about *The Simpsons* arcade game (Chapter 1), highlighting contemporaries such as *Teenage Mutant Ninja Turtles* and noting that the emergence of *Street Fighter II* and the fighting game genre altered the course of popular arcade games in the nineties. They were certainly the arcade games that called to me as I whiled away my middle school afternoons at local pizza arcades in suburban Los Angeles. Fighting games weren't the only arcade games available in the last decade of the twentieth century, but they were by far the most common and lucrative. I kept up with the arcade fighting games for a while, but home consoles were capable of matching the arcade experience by the late nineties and I became more interested in saving my money for the PlayStation and Nintendo 64 titles of the time.

The Simpsons Bowling was released at the end of this era, and it's one of those games that I was surprised to discover years after its initial release. I eventually learned of the existence of the game as I researched the catalogue of *Simpsons* games in the early aughts, but the closest I got to experiencing the game myself was old online articles, screenshots, and subpar game emulation. It wasn't until 2005 that I finally found a cabinet and played the game as it was meant to be played. And it wasn't in some neighborhood arcade or bowling alley, but the break room at Vivendi Games. The company was formed from the rubble of what used to be Fox Interactive, and this machine had come along for the merger. I'd been working there for a year or so and had just moved to a different floor of the building where I discovered the arcade in a far corner, never played and always set to free play. It didn't take much play time to get the gist of the game, but it was a neat work bonus just the same.

Incidentally, the office for Vivendi Games—before its closure in 2008—was located right down the street from the arcades I frequented as a teenager. It felt like a nice bit of closure to my days as an arcade fiend.

Skipping work for the sport of kings.

The Simpsons were a notable absence in the video game scene at the end of the twentieth century. *Virtual Springfield* released on Windows and Macintosh in 1997, and outside of a small LCD handheld game in 1999 from Tiger Electronics, the Simpsons made no game appearances for a few years. *Virtual Springfield* sold close to two hundred thousand units—or about five million dollars—but those numbers didn't make for a blockbuster hit by then, and especially not for a company like Fox that was trying to establish themselves as a serious competitor in the game industry. So things went silent again as Fox figured out what to do with *The Simpsons* in video games.

But they didn't go dark on all fronts. Fox Interactive continued to publish video games in earnest through the late nineties with Fox properties such as *Independence Day*, *Aliens vs. Predator*, and *The X-Files*, in addition to original titles like the action-platformer *Croc* series. These were all home releases for consoles and PC, with nary a care for arcades. While established arcade manufacturers like Capcom and Sega could continue to turn a profit from developing new arcade titles, young guns like Fox Interactive didn't have the infrastructure, nor probably the appetite, to try and enter that market. At least, not on their own.

Fox Interactive finally entered the arcade market in partnership with their old friend, the developer of the game many people regard as the best *Simpsons* game of all time: Konami. We haven't seen them in the picture since *The Simpsons* arcade game and a few PC titles in 1991, but someone decided they'd be a great developer for the first *Simpsons* game to hit arcades in a decade. The circumstances had changed for Konami since those days. Instead of getting a development team from their headquarters in Japan, Fox Interactive worked with the team at Konami Amusement of America—or KAA—to develop this unique title based on a sport that is most popular in the States. In fact, Konami would be both publisher and developer of record for the game, with Fox Interactive primarily serving as creative producer for the art, writing, and voice cast. KAA only published a few titles independently of their parent company in Japan, so it seems to have been an experimental time for the American arm of their arcade operations.

However it went down, *The Simpsons Bowling* hit arcades in the summer of 2000 and was the first of a flurry of *Simpsons* games released in a span of four years. It was a time that coincided with Fox's reinvestment in *Simpsons* merchandise, harkening back to those early days of a Simpson plastered on every coffee mug and sitting on every video game shelf. So as always, we can thank Sweet Lady Greed for the re-emergence of *The Simpsons* in video games.

I choose you, Apu!

Arcade aficionados were no strangers to bowling arcade games by the year 2000. Video arcade games with trackball controllers had been around since the late seventies, and while they've become more elaborate in their representations with alleys and bowling accoutrement thrown into the mix, they've generally been about positioning an on-screen bowler or bowling ball from a behind-the-back point of view, then rolling a trackball forward to launch the ball toward the pins. *The Simpsons Bowling* is based on the same design and simply adds a veneer of *Simpsons* goofiness to it.

That "slap the Simpsons on it" attitude represented a notable shift in the marketing strategy for video games starring Our Favorite Family. The show had been in production for ten years by the time this game was released, with many characters on the show taking starring roles alongside the core family members. Characters like Apu, Mr. Burns, Krusty the clown, and Willie the groundskeeper had emerged alongside dozens of others as vital members of the Springfield ensemble, and Fox Interactive realized that the video games were more fun when they threw in as many playable characters and dialogue as possible. So they did just that with *The Simpsons Bowling*, adding the aforementioned characters along with Homer, Marge, Bart, and Lisa to round out the cast of eight playable characters (including Grampa as a secret playable character).[1] Each character came equipped with a bushel of jokes and scenes that played out during character selection, during bowling, and in the final scenes after the game is over. As previously shown, media technology now allowed developers of *Simpsons* video games to take advantage of the voice cast and writers to really punch up the quality of the games. More often than not, that was the highlight of a *Simpsons* game in this era.

Mmm... sports terminology.

The premise of the game is as simple as I described above. There is no side narrative or goal beyond playing the game to win. The player and up to three friends choose to play a normal game or spares game, with the spares mode simply a cycle of spare pin setups to see who can get the most cash (in-game points). The normal mode plays like a standard game in which players take turns hurling the ball along a bowling alley to the pins waiting at the end. Players can roll the ball twice in one frame to knock down the ten pins. If the ten pins are knocked over in one roll it is called a strike, but getting a strike means the scores of the next two rolls are added to the strike. If it takes two rolls to knock down ten pins it is called a spare. The player gets ten points plus extra points from the next roll. Players continue playing for ten frames. The one who knocks out the most pins has the highest score, and therefore wins the game. It's some tricky math but unlike an actual trip to the bowling alley, the game calculates everything for the player.

Once a mode is selected, the player can choose one of the several bowlers, each with their own rating in Power, Straight rolls, and Curved rolls. Some characters have a healthy balance of the three qualities, while others are higher in one rating at the cost of the other two. Willie, for example, has a whopping 9.5 out of 10 rating for both Power and Straight rolls, but his Curved rolls are rated at a lowly 4 out of 10. This puts a Willie player in a tough spot if they need a curved roll to nail a spare or make a tricky roll. But it ultimately doesn't matter too much in a light-hearted game like this. It's clearly not meant to be a deep simulation of the bowling experience. It's more like a drunken bowling hangout with some friends.

Bend your knees, spread your legs, back straight.

The actual bowling gameplay is just a few steps. First, the player rolls the trackball left or right to set the curve for the ball, which can help in causing pins to scatter in a beneficial pattern, or to hit those aforementioned annoying spares. Next, they move the character left and right to position them accordingly, then hit the button next to the trackball to step forward. Finally, it's time to wait for a meter on the side to be in the green zone and roll the ball at the right time to get an optimal roll. Players will occasionally unlock special balls after scoring three strikes in a row, and although there are no extra points for using one, they look pretty cool. The special balls are a flaming bowling ball, Maggie Simpson herself (babies make great bowling balls!?), a ball full of nuclear sludge, and a bomb ball that causes a big explosion. This is the most fun to watch. Each roll comes with those short character moments I mentioned and, unless someone is a die-hard bowling fan, they'll probably enjoy those the most.

In addition to the dialogue, the art and animation took a major leap forward with the first 3D representation of the characters in a video game. While *The Simpsons* hasn't always shined in 3D video games, this first attempt did a decent job of showcasing the characters' designs and personalities. The bowling alley was also notably a 3D space, but there are numerous elements that are shown as 2D textures instead. The characters that appear in the background are as flat as cardboard cutouts at a shooting gallery. But they're meant to be just set dressing. Some of the playable characters come with a spiffy bowling shirt redesign and goofy animation to match their actions and dialogue. The biggest bummer of the art is how empty the whole place feels. It would have been nice to see other characters bowling in the adjacent lanes and for all active players to be shown seated around the lane as well. They're nits to pick in a game that's simple but solid.

The power of the special arson ball.

The Simpsons Bowling is the first of these arcade-type games that are light on narrative and meant to be a pure dialogue and joke delivery system. It's the kind of design I went on about in earlier chapters, but now we see another finger curl on the monkey's paw. The characters and voices are there, but without a narrative it all feels flat and an awful lot like those greedy cash-grabs I've been joking about. So we need more than just a *Simpsons* joke book in a video game. We need the characters to have a reason for being there. *The Simpsons* television show did this to great success with the "Team Homer" episode from season seven in which Homer and his friends form a bowling team and trick Mr. Burns into sponsoring the team, after which he demands to join them and tanks their winning streak. It was certainly this episode that inspired *The Simpsons Bowling*, and some of the characters even wear their bowling shirts from the episode.

Winner gets to grease up Willie.

This is certainly an oddball in the *Simpsons* game catalogue. *The Simpsons Bowling* is not nearly as memorable or highly regarded as the original beat 'em up classic from 1990, and the unique technical specs such as reliance on now-ancient CD-ROM drives make it a hassle and a half to emulate properly, not to mention a pain to maintain for a real cabinet. Heck, the emulated version of the game doesn't even have voices, and that pretty much makes it a pointless endeavor. The machines are scattered about and still maintained by enthusiasts, but it's getting harder to find (though I was lucky enough to find one in Hillsboro, Oregon).[2] I'd say it's worth a dollar or two to roll a few balls and see what the fuss is about. Unless Konami or Fox Interactive are convinced to bring it back in some digital form, this may very well become the rarest *Simpsons* video game of all time.

Notes

1. "MAME The Simpsons Bowling (Perfect Game, Grampa)" (YouTube, 2021). Archived on youtube.com by bubufubu. Retrieved 21 March 2021.
2. Next Level Pinball Shop & Museum. 1458 NE 25th, Hillsboro, Oregon, USA. Visited 19 October 2019.

Chapter 16: The Assorted Horrors

Night of the Living Treehouse of Horror - March 2001

I've established that I joined the legions of fans whose comedic sensibilities were shaped by the antics of a town full of dopes and their cynical brand of humor. And while I enjoy the classic episodes as much as anyone who grew up with them, I'm also in that fan club of people who were especially delighted by the annual Halloween specials, collectively known as the "Treehouse of Horror" series. These horror-themed episodes began as parodies of the horror and science fiction films and television series that the writers grew up with in the sixties and seventies. Older viewers may understand and appreciate the references to shows such as *The Twilight Zone* and *Night Gallery*, but children of the nineties were unlikely to get those jokes behind the jokes. It's a testament to the quality of the show that these classic parodies retold through the medium of *The Simpsons* could still feel like funny, original stories that introduced a new generation of viewers to horror and science fiction of a different era. The source material evolved as the show progressed through the decades, moving ahead to more recent material such as the supernatural teen angst from *Twilight* or the technology angst from *Black Mirror*.

The structure of each "Treehouse of Horror" episode has remained unchanged for over thirty years. Sometime around Halloween (and even one Thanksgiving), *The Simpsons* premieres an episode consisting of three short tales of terror. These comedic takes on popular stories wedge the characters from the show into the narrative, packing in the mile-a-minute jokes and references that audiences have come to expect. Some episodes feature a wraparound or introductory segment as a framing story for the shorts, but the majority of the episodes are simply three short stories presented in the span of twenty-two minutes. The episodes are difficult to produce, requiring extra work from the writers and a higher budget for art and animation, given that these episodes introduce new character designs, backgrounds, and sometimes even a change in the style of animation. "Treehouse of Horror VI" famously produced a short called "Homer³" in which Homer and Bart enter a world visualized as a 3D wonderland, with characters themselves rendered as 3D models for the first time in the series's history. It was a groundbreaking event for a primetime television show in 1995, and it joined other notable 3D pioneers like *Toy Story* and the *ReBoot* animated series in introducing computer generated animation to the masses.

I personally loved all of these episodes, and even though I stopped keeping pace with the release of the regular series, I continue to watch the "Treehouse of Horror" specials each Halloween. It's perhaps no surprise that I became as interested in these video games as I did. The video games are simply variations on the same theme: bizarre collections of stories in which characters from the show get super powers, fight aliens and monsters, and travel through twisted versions of the reality of the show. It took a while, but video game developers eventually realized that combining the "Treehouse of Horror" episodes and video games was a perfect fit.

Bart's just thinking of a dirty joke.

Fox Interactive made a distinct change to their business model after a few years of operation in the late nineties. They retained their position within the greater

Fox entity as the division that focused on video games, but they stopped trying to be the sole publisher. *Virtual Springfield* from 1997 remained their sole credit as publisher of record for a *Simpsons* game. As we saw with *The Simpsons Bowling*, Fox Interactive had transformed to become more of a caretaker of the license. They provided direction and eased the licensing hurdles between the game publisher and Gracie Films, which had taken on a greater role in reviewing and approving the design of video games based on *The Simpsons*.

The early aughts saw Fox Interactive take a different approach from their predecessors in the early nineties. Instead of working with one publisher, they diversified, establishing relationships with multiple publishing partners and signing deals for a game at a time instead of multi-title deals that locked them into extended partnerships. We saw the drawback of this approach when Fox allowed Acclaim to publish their *Simpsons* games for four years. Few of their games achieved critical success, and sales were only as strong as the hype of Simpsonsmania. *The Simpsons* was a decade old by the year 2000 and a change in strategy was necessary for video game merchandise based on such a well-established but settled property.

Fox Interactive also seemed interested in what some might consider non-essential platforms for a video game business. Perhaps Fox Interactive was so risk averse that they thought it would be better to release games onto established platforms instead of investing in development for next-gen hardware. *The Simpsons Bowling* released in arcades at a time when arcade popularity focused on fighting games and dance simulators. At the same time, they signed deals with additional publishers for games set to release on home platforms in 2001. The first of these home releases was with THQ as publisher for a game on the aging Game Boy Color and featuring designs based on those "Treehouse of Horror" shorts.

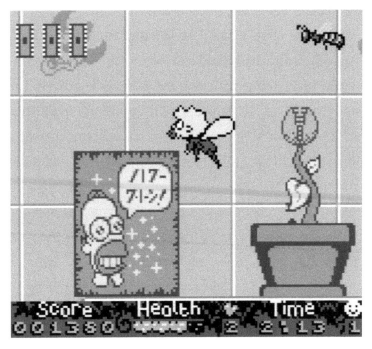

Life ain't easy for a fly.

THQ was a well-established company by 2001. Initially founded in 1990 as a toy company, THQ radically shifted their business by the mid-nineties, focusing on video games entirely. They were known as an aggressive competitor who acquired a variety of development studios to develop properties such as *Destroy All Humans!*, *Darksiders*, and *Saints Row*. They were also a major presence in the licensed game field, with multiple sports contracts and too many licensed cartoon games under their belt to name. One notable license they held was the *Rugrats* cartoon from Nickelodeon, and the company they worked with to develop these games has already appeared before on a *Simpsons* title: Software Creations.

Software Creations previously appeared as the developer of the 1994 dud for the original Game Boy called *Bart and the Beanstalk* (Chapter 10). While a competent platformer, the game was bereft of *Simpsons* designs and had little to distinguish it from a generic game based on the fairy tale of Jack and the beanstalk. Software Creations continued to till the licensed game soil in the six years since they worked on *Bart and the Beanstalk*, including development of the aforementioned *Rugrats* game series across Game Boy, Game Boy Color, and Game Boy Advance. While none of the developers from *Bart and the Beanstalk* appear in the credits of *Night of the Living Treehouse of Horror*, there are numerous names from the *Rugrats* games that do appear. The similarities don't end with the credits. When comparing *Night of the Living Treehouse of Horror* to the *Rugrats* games by Software Creations, it's clear that the designers already had a pipeline in place for churning out these games, including reuse of assets and fonts so they wouldn't have to start from scratch. More than one of the *Rugrats* games has art that appears in *Night of the Living Treehouse of Horror*. This isn't necessarily a bad thing and I'm sure the efficiency of reusing art allowed them to create the game on a tight budget, but it does make for some generic designs that don't all fit the world of *The Simpsons*.

However they achieved it, Software Creations was all wrapped up with the game by early 2001. THQ released a few images and some information to tease the game but otherwise didn't do much marketing, and the game released in March of 2001 to positive reviews. It went on to sell a quarter of a million units, which wasn't bad for a small game on the Game Boy Color. That may be why we'll see THQ pop up again in the future. Software Creations, however, was purchased by that old stalwart of the industry, our greedy old corporate pal—Acclaim. They were renamed Acclaim Studios Manchester and survived long enough to be shuttered as part of Acclaim's bankruptcy in 2004. This was their last *Simpsons* game.

Bart surveils his handiwork.

All that history brings us that which Software Creations has wrought. For all its baggage, *Night of the Living Treehouse of Horror* is a refreshing take on a 2D *Simpsons* game with varying gameplay between levels. And for the first time, the entire family is playable in a story-driven game. (Light as that story may be). The premise sees the Simpson family's souls trapped in the titular treehouse of horror after falling asleep from eating too much candy, and each of them must escape their respective nightmares in order to proceed to the end of the night and escape the treehouse. The story and gameplay for each of the game's seven levels is themed around a particular "Treehouse of

Horror" short, with clearly identifiable links to the source material. It's the first time a *Simpsons* game so literally translates episodes of the show to a video game, while still introducing new elements that must have been required in order to lay out a complete level.

Gameplay varies by level, though one broad note for all levels is the game's unfortunate lag. The controls are just a bit slow, with button presses taking precious milliseconds to process and perform the intended action. It can manifest as a distraction to the gameplay in the levels where characters need to jump to avoid being hit by enemies. It certainly ain't no *Super Mario Bros.*, which is a lesson no *Simpsons* game developer ever seemed to learn. If you're going to make a platformer, follow the best of the bunch. But knowing that this game is built on the tech they developed for *Rugrats*, perhaps it's an unfortunate restriction. One clearly common element with the *Rugrats* series is the camera's design. While many 2D games keep the player character in the center of the screen, the *Rugrats* titles shift the camera toward the direction that the player is facing. It can feel a bit disconcerting and perhaps nausea-inducing for some players, but obviously makes it easier to look ahead on a screen limited to a resolution of 160 by 144 pixels. *Night of the Living Treehouse Horror* keeps the same camera trick and considering some of the tricky jumps, it's nice to have the extra visibility. And if players just can't get through the

234

game's drudgery, they have the option to adjust the difficulty in the Options menu at the start of the game.

The game's art is noticeably crude, with text fonts that look a bit slapdash and character sprites that aren't quite on-model. However, compared to the previous entries in the 2D *Simpsons* game lineage, this is a work of art. The developers' pedigree with the *Rugrats* series clearly inspired many of the game's visual designs, especially those that weren't tied to a particular *Simpsons* location. Homer's journey through Mr. Burns's castle, for example, looks nothing like the castle that appears on the television episode, but it still looks quite good, capturing the feel of a *Castlevania* level's dark and spooky atmosphere. Other levels are more faithfully designed, like Lisa's journey through Springfield Elementary consisting of hallways and classrooms that do look like those on the show.

The game also updates the old 2D platformer formula by introducing a password system that allows players to resume progress from a given level when they enter the correct password. The password system in video games was very old hat by 2001, so it certainly feels dated, but it's a step that at least gives the player the opportunity to skip to their favorite levels. It was also undoubtedly designed as a cost-saving measure, since save files require extra programming time and a battery on the cartridge, all of which could add up to significant costs for a project that was obviously lean on the budget.

Giant donuts attract the wrong crowd.

The first level eases the player into the game with "Bad Dream House," a 2D platformer level inspired by the story of the same title from the first "Treehouse of Horror" episode in 1990. But unlike the majority of these rote platformers, this level requires the player to explore the titular haunted house in order to find fuses that light up rooms in the house, and that in turn allows players to collect all the keys necessary to reach the attic and save Santa's Little Helper, the family dog. Players face enemies in all areas and a tight timer, which is a feature in all levels. However, Bart is equipped with a slingshot that does help clear out enemies... at least those in the lit areas.

The unlit rooms contain a ghostly broom enemy that shows no quarter in its attack of the player, and this broom actually reappears in the attic as the final boss. It's all straightforward in hindsight, but first-time players will undoubtedly struggle to figure out the order of events to light up rooms, as well as the slingshot's tricky aiming. This level also reintroduces another common problem with the 2D *Simpsons* games: ear-splitting music. The tinny, forever repeating *Simpsons* theme song appears again here, making the audio a grating trap that most of the levels lead the player into. It's wise to have other tunes in the background while playing through the level.

The next level is a respite from jumping in "Flying Tonight," a level based on the "Fly vs. Fly" story from the 1997 episode "Treehouse of Horror VIII." That's also the latest episode to be featured in the game, ensuring that all the levels are derived from episodes in the so-called golden era. This story saw Bart turning into a mutant with the body of a fly and his own head, whereas his human body saw itself topped by a giant fly's head. They flip the script in this level by introducing Maggie as the playable character, her first outing as anything other than art in a cinematic or background. The gameplay involves maneuvering Maggie-Fly from a 2D side view through a kitchen fraught with perils such as wasps, steam from a stove, and electric bug zappers. And like the previous level, Maggie must complete various objectives before proceeding into the teleporter at the end. The player must gather three microchips required to fix said teleporter, as well as flip various switches in order to deactivate the steam vent and proceed. The level is notably easier and shorter than the previous level, and there isn't even a boss at the end. It's a bit of a breather in a game filled with challenging levels.

Eat book.

Marge makes her only appearance in the third level, "Plan 9 From Outer Springfield." Based on the popular tale of "Dial 'Z' For Zombies" from "Treehouse of Horror III," this level changes to an overhead isometric perspective to fully embrace shooting hordes of the undead. Marge shoots her way toward the top of the

238

screen in gameplay reminiscent of classics like Capcom's *Commando* and countless other shoot 'em up games in which the player controls a ship instead of a person. Marge is equipped with a nondescript cannon and unlimited ammo, and she can also pick up fertilizer and water upgrades to give her shots some extra oomph against the zombies. The player must proceed through the Evergreen Terrace neighborhood dodging regular zombies and fighting zombified versions of Springfield denizens Apu, Moe Syzlak, Principal Skinner, and Krusty the clown. Each boss fight features the characters shooting Marge with their respective weapons just like Marge shoots them, but each fight's pattern is progressively more difficult until the final fight against Krusty at the Simpson house. It's a relatively short level when players realize they can just dodge all the regular zombies and focus their attention and ammo on the bosses.

Homer must have had a particularly bad piece of nougat because he's the playable character of three out of the game's seven nightmares. The fourth level sees him in a *Castlevania*-esque quest to defeat the vampire lord Mr. Burns in "Vlad All Over," a take on the classic vampire story from "Bart Simpson's Dracula" in "Treehouse of Horror IV." The game returns to 2D platforming and even gives Homer a crossbow that works just like Bart's slingshot in the first level, although it's not nearly as useful. Most of the enemies cannot be hurt by the weapon, and its only real use is in taking out annoying bats and other creatures that stand in the way. The castle's guards and living statues must simply be dodged in order to proceed. The castle itself has its own devilish machinations that require the player to hit switches that unlock doors leading to other doors. It's a confusing design choice that does stretch out the time it takes to get through the level. The castle's other hazards include a section in which deadly vines rise from the ground and constantly nip at Homer's heels as the player tries to jump over them, and the castle's outdoor section is a gauntlet of arrows and spear-toting guards that can drive one mad. The one offensive weapon at the player's disposal is inexplicably taken away during the boss fight against Mr. Burns. However, when players figure out that they only need to open the overhead windows to let in the sunlight, it becomes less of a boss fight and more of a vampire corral.

It's time for employee reviews.

Homer's nightmare continues in "If I Only Had a Body," a level in which Homer's head is placed on a robot body as part of Mr. Burns's efforts to stop wasting money on useless things like human employees. The original tale, featured in "If I Only Had a Brain" from Treehouse of Horror II, saw Homer's brain placed into a robotic skull, but in this instance he's been completely dismembered and must journey through the Springfield Nuclear Power Plant to recover his arms, legs, and torso. Homer has no weapons here and can only jump over the power plant workers who are out to stop him. The body parts are hidden in things like barrels and fire extinguishers and

241

require the player to actively search for them until they find a body part, represented as a bone. Once a part is collected, it must be returned to the surgery table where the level began before they can search for more parts to complete the level.

Lisa tags in for a stealth mission against cannibalistic teachers in "Nightmare Cafeteria," based on the story of the same title from "Treehouse of Horror V." Unlike the original tale in which no one survives, Lisa takes the proactive approach in this level and sets out to save five of the children who are waiting in cages to be preyed upon by hungry teachers and school personnel. Lisa can't attack anyone, and instead relies on her ability to, um, press against a wall. This stealth mechanic allows the player to press a button when Lisa's in front of a flat wall to make her invisible to the teachers who can't be bothered to turn to the side. Using this ability, players must explore the school hallways and classrooms to find the keys that unlock the cages, then seek out the correct cage for each key to free the five children. The teachers who patrol the hallways chase after Lisa if they spot her and can only be avoided by ducking into a different room. It plays similarly to the first level, and handy trackers in the top-left portion of the screen make it easy to track progress through the level.

The final level brings back Homer for a final round of horror in "King Homer." This level is based on the story from "Treehouse of Horror III" that plays as a parody of

King Kong, with Homer as the titular King Homer. It's also an interesting reversal from the level in 1994's *Virtual Bart* where Bart is a kaiju on a rampage and must battle King Homer at the end. This time, Homer is the protagonist who must charge through town and destroy all tanks and airplanes that dare to mess with him. Players will also recognize a stark similarity to the fists-and-fury gameplay in that classic Atari franchise, *Rampage*. The level is designed for the player to traverse the side-scrolling level while destroying as much as possible until they reach the skyscraper on the far right. There, they must dodge attacks from airplane fire and fight them off as the final boss. Once cleared, King Homer proceeds to the top of the building to play yo-yo with his beloved Marge. (Not a euphemism.)

Oh yeah, there's a dog in this family.

The game's rough edges make it difficult to recommend to anyone but the most faithful *Simpsons* devotees or someone who's already played the far more fun fare on Game Boy Color. I say this knowing that this is also one of the best 2D side-scrollers in the *Simpsons* game oeuvre, besting many of the games featured earlier in this book. I only wish Software Creations had the same luxury that they had with the *Rugrats* series: a chance to make multiple games. Those games showed that, over time, they were able to refine their designs, add more content, and introduce a wider variety of gameplay. Unfortunately, the Game Boy Color was at the end of its life by 2001, and Software Creations wouldn't last much longer either. It's another example of the Simpsons getting short shrift in their efforts to do well on home platforms.

Chapter 17: The Thunderbolts from Heaven

The Simpsons Wrestling - April 2001

Disappointment. Do you remember it, that first sense of something having profoundly let you down? People often do, though we must try our best to forgive them. Politicians make it part of their lifetime vocations. And entertainment, why, I'd say we expect it. Every piece of media, every work of art, has the potential to just bomb and let us down. Something that's free may not sting, but when it costs money, hoo boy.

Such was the case with my first purchase of a video game based on *The Simpsons*. As I mentioned before, I loved the television show, but didn't come around to the video games until much later. The way I figure it, I didn't have the disposable income necessary to bet on a *Simpsons* game during the 16-bit era, and then didn't have a PC during the time when *Virtual Springfield* was in stores. It wasn't until 2001—my senior year of high school—when I finally had money and a willingness to buy a *Simpsons* game based on name alone. I don't exactly recall where I bought a PlayStation video game in the year our of lord 2001 (likely at the Gamestop in the Fox Hills Mall), but I remember powering through the game's wrestling circuits, playing in two player mode with my brothers, and realizing "Oh, this is bad." The bitter taste lingers to this day.

Shut up ref, a burp cloud is totally legal.

The new millennium kicked off a game of musical chairs with different publishers shuffling the *Simpsons* license between them. Konami started things off, then THQ for their Game Boy Color entry, and now Activision. This fervent pimping of the license was perhaps a desire on Fox's part to vary the publishers and types of games associated with the license after a decade of being stuck with only one or two game makers. Or, and probably more likely, they were out to diversify their sources of video

247

game cash during their renewed wave of *Simpsons* merchandising.

Fox Interactive had some publisher duties on their games at this time, but they were still scared to go it alone and brought in Activision to distribute. This was Activision's first and last go at the *Simpsons* license. The company was, of course, a behemoth in the industry by the early aughts. After being founded by David Crane (who we met back in the NES and Game Boy era) and other former Atari employees, the company met early success with titles such as *Pitfall!* on the Atari 2600 selling millions of cartridges before the video game industry crashed around 1983. Activision scraped by in the eighties and was eventually purchased by a group of investors including Bobby Kotick, who fired nearly everyone and rebuilt the company to become a profit-driven game factory. To their credit, Activision's development studios were putting out interesting games such as *Vigilante 8* and *Tony Hawk's Pro Skater* at this time, although Activision wouldn't rely on any of their internal studios for their newly acquired *Simpsons* agreement. Instead, they turned to a studio primarily known for their license collaborations with LucasArts: Big Ape Productions.

Big Ape was a fresh-faced kid relative to all the other parties involved. Founded by game designers Mike Ebert and Dean Sharpe after working on *Zombies Ate My Neighbors* and *Metal Warriors* at LucasArts, the company's first game shipped in 1997 for both PlayStation and Sega

Saturn. Though working at their own company, the new project—a Grecian adventure tale dubbed *Herc's Adventures*—was once again published by LucasArts because why shop around for a developer when you can just do nepotism? The game is now considered a cult classic from the height of the PlayStation's reign, although interestingly not a 3D showcase at a time when 3D was all the rage. This changed when Big Ape worked with LucasArts again to develop the game adaptation of *Star Wars Episode I: The Phantom Menace* in 1999. This clunky 3D action-adventure game was actually a fair match for the clunky pace of the movie, and although it's not a highly regarded game in the *Star Wars* franchise, it still had some interesting sequences. This second collaboration with LucasArts was also the last, and Big Ape moved on to work exclusively on licensed fare for the remainder of their brief existence. *The Simpsons Wrestling* followed in 2001 on the distinctly aged PlayStation platform, then a final chance to flex their wrestling muscles with the PlayStation 2 version of *MTV Celebrity Deathmatch* in 2003. The company shuttered in 2003 with licensed wrestling games quietly ending their time in the game industry. *Herc's Adventures* remains their most notable title.

One other notable credit is the final appearance of Jamie Angell as dialogue writer. He fell into a rapid succession of games based on *The Simpsons*, with all three of his credits (*The Simpsons Bowling*, *Night of the Living*

Treehouse of Horror, and *The Simpsons Wrestling*) releasing within a year of each other. In the early days, it felt like writing was a crucial aspect of the show that was entirely missing. Angell, a writer of some of the *Simpsons* comics from Bongo as well, was finally bringing a professional hand to the characters' voices. In fact, according to Big Ape designer Mike Ebert, it sometimes wasn't quite what they were looking for, with some lines described as "too graphic and offensive for games."[1] It's worth noting that while Angell was contributing dialogue and in-game text for the games, he wasn't developing stories. Looking at the stories of these games, it's clear they were at best light, at worst a flimsy excuse for characters to compete against one another and throw out some zingers for the fans. The publishers of these games were banking on character appeal selling copies to players, much like they expected Bart's face on a mug to sell. Nonetheless, it was a step in the right direction, and we'd see what a fully developed story-based *Simpsons* game looks like just a few years later.

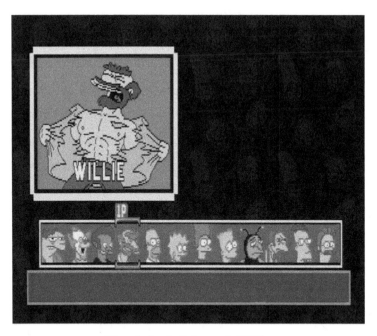

My advice is DO touch Willie.

Televised wrestling hit a certain stride in the late nineties. The WWF—World Wrestling Federation—entered its Attitude Era and changed the brand from family-friendly and patriotic athletic displays to adult-oriented stories about rivalries and betrayal. In other words, they aged up wrestling to keep up with the aging demographic. They also brought wrestling back to network television via the successful *Smackdown* program on the UPN channel. This all served to stir up excitement about wrestling again and brought it into the video game realm with hits such as 1998's *WWF War Zone*. Wrestling was simply in the air and Big Ape caught a whiff.

The Simpsons Wrestling is set up as a tournament-based fighting game with two characters facing off in a best-of-three match. The player selects a wrestler from a starting cast of eight characters: Homer, Bart, Lisa, Marge, Barney, Krusty, Apu, and Willie. Not content to stop there, an additional eight characters can be unlocked by completing the game's circuit challenges: Bumblebee Man, Moe, Professor Frink, Flanders, Smithers, Kang, Itchy, and Scratchy. That's a hell of a turn-out and it speaks to the focus of this game's design. The designers decided that the reward for playing a game featuring the cast of *The Simpsons* is not the story, or even necessarily the jokes, but the characters themselves. You're just here to see Barney and listen to him burp, right? Or to hear him tell you that he's "going to jump all over you like brown on beer."

Anime freeze frame... now!

The characters do more than hurl quips at each other (though that can be fun in the right circumstances).[2] All wrestlers (and I use that term loosely) possess the same basic set of abilities for whomping each other. They can jump about twelve feet in the air, punch and kick, throw ranged weapons and special attacks, and pin each other when health is low enough. They also have a couple of unique powerful attacks and taunts that can be unleashed when a character's stamina bar is sufficiently filled. They all move at roughly the same speeds, so choice of character comes down to a player's favorite or a need to beat a particularly powerful opponent. For example, the whole wrestling tournament is orchestrated by the aliens Kang and Kodos for... reasons, and Kang is the final match of each circuit. They are tough to beat, but certain characters are so obviously overpowered that it only makes sense to select them for such tough wrestling matches. Flanders is the prime example. He possesses a special attack during which he summons the wrath of God to repeatedly shoot lightning down on his opponent, inflicting massive damage in the process. Flanders also has the holy ability to revive after being pinned, effectively doubling the time required to beat him and keep him pinned. Beyond the unbalanced design of some characters, there was also the inevitable reliance on jump kicks to an opponent's head, an annoying but effective spam maneuver that inflicted significant damage.

I could continue to gripe about the poor sense of balance between the characters' strengths and weaknesses, but again, I don't think the developers were focused on that at all. They clearly thought it would be fun to make some characters too powerful for a normal match, and knew no serious fighting game fan would play this for real competition. They also had no qualms about pitting adults against children like Bart and Lisa. There's nothing quite like seeing Homer Simpson beat up and pin down his own children. Interestingly, Fox had some thoughts on the game's original level of violence. Mike Ebert recalls the lesson: "Be sure the licensee is aware of the violence level of the game. It's really hard after the game is at Alpha to go back and make it so some characters can not attack others."[3]

You are no match for Willie's pecs.

Gameplay aside, the game's technical aspects are very much of the era. The art features colorful but compromised designs, with both the 3D models and 2D characters that sit like cardboard cutouts on a television set in the background. Each map is centered on a wrestling ring with character art slapped onto it, a cast of said cutouts scattered outside the ring, and backgrounds featuring familiar locales such as the Simpson house and Moe's Tavern. One map you won't see is Springfield Elementary School. Current events required it to be removed, as Ebert notes, "Try to avoid having the 'Columbine Massacre' make you cut levels involving schools."[4] Yes, let's please not have child massacre references.

The visuals might have barely passed muster on the old, bulky CRT televisions of the nineties, but the 256 by 224 pixel resolution doesn't scale up well when played on modern televisions. Couple that with the low resolution art and it's a recipe for one ugly game. This is where we pause to consider that the game shipped two years after the arrival of the PlayStation 2. The first console was such a massive success that it may have made sense to ship the game anyway just to bring in some sales from the millions of PlayStation owners out there, and the game did manage to sell over two hundred thousand copies. As Ebert points out, "If you're going to make a bad game, at least be happy that it made money!"[5] So perhaps it's not fair to complain about visuals in any game on the first PlayStation, but I'll find a way when the source material is so much more vibrant and carefully designed. Granted, it wasn't an easy journey for the developers. As noted above, they faced quite a few challenges. Among them was the loss of their already inexperienced producer midway through the project, removal of features and content at the behest of executives, and just the fact that this "wrestling" game really wasn't a wrestling game at all.[6]

Homer don't play that.

Complain, complain, complain. I do have good news! The CD format of the PlayStation allowed all of the key actors on the cast to go all out with their one-liners, and the voice recordings are exceptional. They even feature the voice of the infamous curmudgeon, Harry Shearer, whose critical roles include Flanders, Smithers, and Mr. Burns. This highlight goes a long way to make a playthrough of the game enjoyable. In addition, a multiplayer mode was thoughtfully added so players could fight against each other and probably get into real fights after spamming overpowered moves to the annoyance of the other player.

The Simpsons Wrestling has the distinction of being one of those games that could have been ported to a variety of platforms if the publisher had faith in the game. Its sole outing on the PlayStation at such a late stage of the console's life tells the tale, and other such *Simpsons* games remain on the horizon.

Notes

1. Michael Ebert, "Other Games" (2021). Retrieved 21 March 2021.
2. "The Secret of Monkey Island's Insult Swordfighting - Here's A Thing" (YouTube, 2017). Archived by Eurogamer on youtube.com. Retrieved 21 March 2021.
3. Michael Ebert.
4. Ibid.
5. Ibid.
6. Ibid.

Chapter 18: The Crazy Lawsuit

The Simpsons Road Rage - November 2001

The year 2001 was a tumultuous one. In the realm of video games, the PlayStation 2 had already been available for a year, and Nintendo's next system—the Gamecube—was due to release at the end of the year alongside a new competitor, Microsoft's Xbox console. Sega's longtime presence in the game hardware industry ended that year when they accepted the commercial failure of the Sega Dreamcast and ceased production, abandoning hardware development to focus on software. It was also perhaps the last significant shift in graphics capabilities, with the PlayStation and Nintendo 64's chunky polygons and blurry textures evolving into the much more eyeball-friendly graphics of a new generation.

It was the year I graduated from high school. I had a part-time job, a car, disposable income, and college loomed on the horizon. I could buy games, hardware, and even a decent PC for the first time. The Internet was in full swing and I was becoming acquainted with people from around the world through the virtues of chat and fansites, not to mention the possibility of simply downloading games instead of having to buy a cartridge or disc from a store. It felt like that rite of passage that so many speak of but often eludes us in the transition to adulthood. The year might have benignly passed us by, but we were in for a shock that no one saw coming. The tragic destruction of the World Trade Center on September 11, 2001 occurred in my first few weeks of college. The first class to resume after the attack was my public speaking class, and instead of making presentations about movies, personal goals, or even video games as I might have done, most of the class discussed loved ones or friends of friends who perished in the attack. Most students wept or sulked. It was the first sense of vulnerability for many of us.

Companies marched on with their entertainment products, patriotically obeying president George Bush when he warned that we shouldn't allow America to become a place "where we don't conduct business, where people don't shop."[1] Some movies, games, and television shows delayed their releases if their content was too close to reality, but by the end of year, we still had those new consoles to focus on. If anything, video games served a purpose they would often find in times of tragedy. An escape, a release from the challenge of living through dark times.

But the video game future was bright indeed. Of the three next generation consoles available by the end of year, I only owned the Nintendo Gamecube, which was released in November of 2001. To date, it is the only console I preordered and picked up on launch day, along with a copy of the mouthful that is *Star Wars Rogue*

Squadron II: Rogue Leader. I went to the mall to pick up that preorder in defiance of the doctor's orders after a tonsillectomy, because what better way to pass the convalescence than with a new game console? It remained my only Gamecube game until December, when Electronic Arts released a certain clone of Sega's *Crazy Taxi* series that I never would've looked at if not for its goofy yellow characters.

Please kill him.

As we found out in the last few chapters, *The Simpsons* was back on the merch scene with a variety of licensed products releasing to stores. The strategy was transparently about making as much merchandise with these characters as possible, harkening back to the mania of the early nineties. The show itself was now in its thirteenth season, and well into a period where old fans were bemoaning its drop in quality while other fans transitioned into the period believing it was still a better show than any other comedy on television. The year had already seen a *Simpsons* game on Game Boy Color and another on PlayStation. Releasing games on those platforms were safe bets that did yield some commercial success, with each game selling over two hundred thousand copies, even if the critical response was less than ideal. The question now was what about the next generation? What does a *Simpsons* game mean on the latest and greatest hardware?

It's strange to realize that these games were in development at the same time as *The Simpsons Road Rage*. Each game was published and developed by different companies, with only Fox Interactive serving as the connective tissue between them. One can imagine the rigorous approval process each publisher experienced while preparing their respective releases, but while Fox Interactive would undoubtedly exercise control of the representation of the characters in the video games, it seemed like game quality was left entirely to the publisher and developer. The first two attempts were seen as strikeouts, or at best foul balls. But the third pairing of publisher and developer would be an unexpected home run.

Electronic Arts may have been the publisher of record here, but their creative influence seems to have been minimal. The credits highlight that they provided certain services such as marketing, packaging, and game testing, all of which are common when a publisher takes on distribution duties. As we've seen before, Fox Interactive had become skittish about taking on the risk of product distribution, and it seems likely that they sold distribution rights to Electronic Arts for a percentage of sales. So then, what led them to propose this particular product for distribution? That's where Radical Entertainment comes in.

Enabling Marge's hauling of ass.

Radical Entertainment was a veteran company in the video game industry by 2001. They began life as a game developer a decade earlier, when Distinctive Software employees Rory Armes, Dave Davis, and Ian Wilkinson broke away to form the company. Rory Armes was actually the development producer on *Bart's House of Weirdness* (Chapter 5), and while only Wilkinson remained with Radical when they returned to the license in the early aughts, it's an interesting connection between games that are a decade apart. During their early tenure, the company focused on some licensed games and a wide variety of sports video games such as the *NHL Powerplay* series and *NBA Basketball 2000*. Ironically, this concerted effort to compete in the sports video game market was met by the dominant force of the EA Sports division of Electronic Arts.

Most licensed games of the era began life as a publisher seeking out a developer to develop the license they acquired. However, Radical Entertainment had a different idea. According to Radical designer Joe McGinn, after Radical suffered some losses as projects were cancelled, then-president Wilkinson marched forward with the edict that the company would develop demos and prototypes and use the technology to pitch new types of projects to publishers.[2] The turn of the millennium bears this out as we see sports games from Radical cease in 2001, and the company's output shifted to licensed fare. As McGinn wrote on the Donut Team forum, the pivot "was actually instrumental in getting the *Road Rage* contract, because we had a driving car demo with physics and such running in real time, while our competitors only pitched ideas on paper."[3]

So it was Radical that conceived of *The Simpsons Road Rage* and sold it up the chain. They proved to Fox Interactive that they had the chops to make a fun driving game featuring *The Simpsons*, and they eventually settled on mimicking the gameplay of the *Crazy Taxi* series in which players guide their cabbie around large maps, picking up passengers in exchange for money in a limited amount of time. Fans noticed the similarities, and so did Sega when they decided to file a patent infringement lawsuit against all parties involved to remove *The Simpsons Road Rage* from the shelves and receive the money they were due.[4] The case settled out of court for an undisclosed amount, leaving the question open as to whether they really had a case. The game sold nearly three million copies across the various platforms on which it was released, so it's safe to say that Sega's eyes were full of dollar signs when they realized their gameplay concept was making so much money for someone else.

The fact that it sold so well implies the game was far better than its predecessors, but was it a matter of releasing at the right time on a new generation of consoles, or was the game indeed a renaissance in *Simpsons* game design?

It's more efficient to get dropped off in the middle of an intersection.

In many ways, *The Simpsons Road Rage* is simply a continuation of the type of *Simpsons* game we've seen in this new era. It features the Gang's All Here design in which players have their pick of plenty of characters from the television show beyond just Homer, Marge, Bart, Lisa, and Maggie. In addition to the family, there are twelve Springfield regulars such as Moe and Apu, many of whom must be unlocked by progressing through the game's story. And like *The Simpsons Wrestling*, this format allows the player's selected character to interact with a variety of other Springfieldians, creating many opportunities for characters to drop one-liners and funny conversations. Some of the dialogue also began to match lines you might hear on the more mature-rated television show, such as this, er, gem when Bart picks up Krusty the clown:

Bart: "Krusty! What's up with Springfield's greatest entertainer?"

Krusty: "Plenty, thanks to Viagra!"

The story itself is more of a light premise. Mr. Burns, the ever-reliable evil millionaire of the Springfield universe, purchases the city's mass transit system and immediately dismantles it, replacing the city's buses with nuclear-powered death traps. Lisa rightly declares the buses a "threat to public health," prompting Homer to trigger another Simpsons Did It moment when he pulls an Uber and hires himself out as an unlicensed cabbie for all the citizens who need rides in Springfield. The goal becomes apparent at the first character select screen: Springfield citizens want to earn enough money to buy back the bus system from Mr. Burns for the amount of one million dollars. It's a short introduction and Bart puts the fine point on it when he says "Just get to the game already!"

As noted earlier, the gameplay is more or less lifted straight out of Sega's Crazy Taxi. That game allows players to select a character who must dash about a large city in order to find passengers who are willing to part with some cash in exchange for a ride to a different part of the map. A timer in the corner of the screen means the player has no time for leisurely lollygagging, requiring a certain level of manic racing and destruction to actually reach the destination before the timer runs out. This fast-paced score attack style of car racing was popularized in the first arcade release of *Crazy Taxi* and carried through onto consoles soon after.

Something something evil plot.

If *The Simpsons Road Rage* can be knocked for copying an already existing series, it can be praised for its faithfulness to the source material. The game retains the high frame rate of its inspiration, as well as the responsive controls and physics. Each character's car controls differently from the others, but they are all fun to maneuver across and over the environments, which are themselves designed to be a large-scale playground for car stunts and otherwise impossible feats of vehicular prowess. Some characters' cars are lightweight and fragile but quite easy to zip around in, such as Bart's soapbox racer that originally featured in the third season episode, "Saturdays of Thunder." Other vehicles, such as Reverend Lovejoy's Book Burning Mobile, are slow as molasses but virtual tanks, capable of plowing through traffic on their way to the next drop-off. Like that so-called wrestling game (Chapter 17), only a certain number of characters are available from the start, and unlocking new characters brings improved vehicles along with them, ensuring the player receives a satisfying loop of unlocking new characters and cars that in turn allow for improved drop-off times and better time and cash bonuses for each run through the map.

The car gameplay may be loose and fun, but the environments are there to put a damper on the joy. Each of the game's six locales presents a different area of Springfield, starting with the Evergreen Terrace neighborhood where the Simpsons reside and gradually moving on to other unlockable locales such as Springfield Dam and the Nuclear Power Plant. Like a visit to Disneyland, it can be fun to simply visit these environments and gawk at the familiar names and places. The game even provides a Sunday Drive mode that allows players to leisurely explore the maps without restrictions. While the game's maps are separate and unlocked over time, the designers once dreamed of a single, unified map that allowed players to explore the entire city with no loading times between regions. Video game archivist Liam Robertson interviewed Vlad Ceraldi, technical director on the project, who revealed why they had to remove such a beloved feature:

> The speed of the [PlayStation 2] drives in the retail units were not as efficient or as reliable as the dev units. So, we could not get the data fast enough off the discs in order to populate the world the way we had designed everything.[5]

This problem caused the radical change that led to the game's multiple levels. In addition to tech woes, feedback from Fox and Gracie Films also forced significant changes as development was well underway. Robertson cites game historian Andrew Borman in revealing that the world's art design had a "brighter, more cartoony" look, but that Matt Groening wanted *Road Rage* to "stand apart from the show and look more like a video game."[6]

Hello unaccompanied child, hop in.

Dividing the world into smaller maps created a new set of unlockables for the player, but the maps demand dedication to obtain them all. The standard Road Rage mode requires players to attempt to ferry characters around while facing an intense clutter of cars, trees, rocks, signs, benches, pedestrians, and other objects that sometimes bounce away like beach balls but often just serve to slow down the player car's momentum, ensuring that the player surely but gradually loses time from their run timer, leading to diminishing returns until the player can no longer sustain their progress and ends their run with whatever cash they obtained. There's also the antagonism from Mr. Burns's limousine and his fleet of buses, all of which actively seek out the player to crash into them and sort of bump them around since cars can't actually be destroyed. This cycle of playing through the maps and gathering as much cash as possible is the core loop and can begin to wear on players who don't appreciate the repetitive nature of score attack racing games. Fortunately, the maps also include elements that aid the player in playing as long as possible before time runs out. Playing long enough reveals that character pick-up spots never vary, ensuring that anyone who plays can develop certain routes that prolong a run. The HUD also includes helpful elements such as a radar and a three-dimensional hand that always points the way to the destination.

Lest you think this sounds like a game lacking depth, there are certain strategic factors that promote the long term investment required to actually achieve the game's one million dollar goal and the ending it unlocks. Certain routes between character pick-up spots can be short enough that they may be linked together to create a loop or infinite route, allowing players to beat the level design and actually gather up massive amounts of cash in short periods of time. There are also bonuses to be found by committing acts of destruction, avoiding crashing into anything, and destroying Burns's bus stops. It's not a level of strategy a hardcore player would want, but it's deep enough for a mass market *Simpsons* game.

But there's more to the game than the core Road Rage mode. The Sunday Drive mode mentioned earlier is a fun little practice mode where players can simply wander around the maps and take in the scenery. The Head to Head mode presents an opportunity for two players to compete against each other as they each try to ferry passengers around or even steal passengers from each other. It's not the meatiest multiplayer mode but certainly a fun way to pass time between Road Rage runs. The final mode is a more elaborate and structured set of challenges called Mission Mode. Each of the ten missions presents a specific character and either racing or object destruction challenges. It's a light diversion from the game's primary mode and leads to unlocking The Car Built for Homer, the only unlockable outside of Road Rage mode.

And that's ultimately where the game leads the player. The goal is always to get back to Road Rage mode and keep earning that cash. It's an odd bit of capitalistic gameplay, and although one score is as arbitrary as the next in a video game, the greed aspect is perhaps most fitting for the world of Springfield. Americans' consumerism and enterprising attitude is just the lowest hanging fruit on the mockery tree.

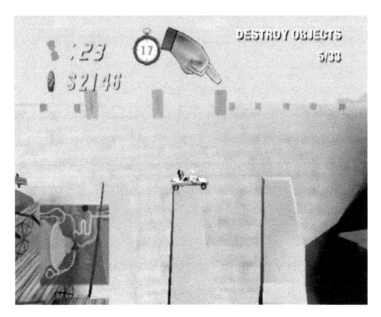

Mid-air drop-offs are not advised.

Players around the world purchased almost 2.5 million copies of *The Simpsons Road Rage* between 2001 and 2005, guaranteeing its success and eventual follow-up. Seeing an opportunity to capitalize on a sure thing, Fox Interactive proceeded to license out the concept to another publisher and developer combo who would bring the game to the Game Boy Advance. THQ returned to take over as publisher for that port and contracted the work to Altron, a Japanese developer for hire that has been in the industry since 1983.

This one *Simpsons* entry on the Game Boy Advance is chock full of visuals reminiscent of the SNES's famed Mode 7 technology, allowing for the illusion of 3D visuals on hardware that couldn't hope to achieve such graphical fidelity. After all, the platform was known as the game system that was keeping the dream of the nineties alive at a time when games were powering forward toward the highest possible 3D fidelity and high definition resolution. This most often resulted in cheaply produced games that yielded decent profits for the investment. *The Simpsons Road Rage* did indeed clear such a bar, selling nearly half a million little cartridges.

Barney's tripping on arcade HUD design.

The gameplay did its best to achieve what succeeded on console, and it was a pretty dang good approximation of the experience. The game is colorful, fast-paced, and includes the same modes as its console parent, including a

Head to Head mode enabled by connecting two GBA systems using the platform's link cable. The one drawback of this port is that it's missing what shines brightest on the more powerful platforms: dialogue and voices. That one critical quality was always missing on those *Simpsons* games from the early nineties, and that limitation is once again present in this throwback to the era. It hurts the enjoyment of the GBA port and perhaps speaks to the superficial nature of most modern *Simpsons* games. They threw in characters, jokes, and voices, and expected that to be enough to bring in sales. It worked out okay in the skilled hands of a developer such as Radical Entertainment, and they would further expand upon their success in just two short years. But a dark cloud still loomed over the Simpsons and their video game appearances... and this cloud rode a skateboard.

Notes

1. "A NATION CHALLENGED; Excerpts From the President's Remarks on the War on Terrorism" (The New York Times, 2001). Archived on nytimes.com. Retrieved 21 March 2021.
2. Joe McGinn, "A Day in the Life: Radical Entertainment" (Donut Team, 2016). Retrieved 21 March 2021.
3. Ibid.
4. David Adams, "SEGA Sues Fox and EA" (IGN, 2003). Retrieved 21 March 2021.

5. Liam Robertson, "The Simpsons Hit & Run's Lost Sequel + Fun Facts – Game History Secrets," *DidYouKnowGaming* (YouTube, 2019). Retrieved 21 March 2021.

6. Ibid.

Chapter 19: The Grind

The Simpsons Skateboarding – November 2002

College is a unique and expensive time in a young person's life. You pay the institution loads of money to ostensibly provide an education that will prepare you for the real world, both in terms of earning potential and molding you into a citizen of the world. But in truth, at least in the United States, it is often just an extension of high school, itself the former source of skills required to live in the world. College "kids" go to class a little more free than they used to be, learning what it means to decide one's course while accruing mile-high debt and still working a part-time job. At least, that's what it was for me.

It was clear that the free high school education I received wouldn't take me anywhere interesting. It seems the more time passes, the higher the bar gets raised. But hey, the diploma counts for something, right? I might have stayed in university if I had the good sense. Instead, in 2002 I decided a university diploma wasn't as important as gaining skills toward the hobby I was most interested in at the time: web design. The Internet was all the rage by then and it seemed like a marketable skill that also just allowed me to do some cool stuff. This was before the era of YouTube where an insightful instructional video is a simple search away. So I left after a year of university to attend one of those once-thriving centers of career acceleration known as vocational colleges, where I'd focus on what they termed "multimedia." Internet, Flash animation, CD-ROMs, oh my!

Oh, did I forget to mention I really just wanted to build fan sites about *The Simpsons*? That's an important detail.

While I developed my web design skills in those terror-filled early aughts, I also joined a few different online communities. GameFAQs was a mainstay as I engaged in writing walkthroughs and learning, well, how to actually write coherent sentences. But I also stumbled across fan sites and forums dedicated entirely to *The Simpsons*. I'd been a fan for a long time, gathering a tiny set of personally recorded VHS tapes that contained my favorite classic episodes. But now I saw an opportunity for a new form of fan expression. I like video games... and almost no one seems to care about video games based on *The Simpsons*... Quite the eureka moment, eh?

So I became That Guy in 2002, embarking on a quest to write walkthroughs for every *Simpsons* game ever made, both for the GameFAQs database but also for my newly created fan site dedicated entirely to those games.[1] It was my niche and I stuck to it even as those *Simpsons* fan communities withered away or transformed into general hangout spots for people who'd become friends, somehow, across an Internet that used to be a lot more wild.

That's an awful lot of words to say that in 2002 I became perhaps the only human being on planet Earth who was genuinely looking forward to something called *The Simpsons Skateboarding*. I was so eager to play it, in fact, that I posted regular updates to my fan site as it was delayed:

> May 15: The date has been pushed all the way to October 1!!! This is ridiculous. EA has yet to make any kind of official announcement about anything in the game, not even a release date. Damn, damn, damn...
>
> November 1: And finally, my bane. My strife. The soul antagonizing element in my life that is driving me insane and causes me to have violent, pillow-pounding dreams... EA has once again delayed *The Simpsons Skateboarding*.

Damn indeed.

The game was eventually released later in November. But how did this ill-timed cash grab come to be?

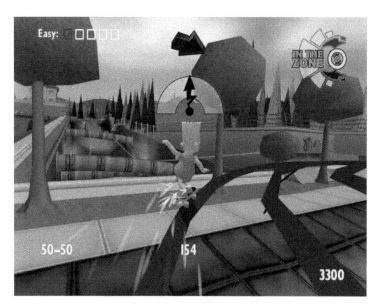

Grinding uphill both ways.

The Simpsons Road Rage burned rubber all over its creators' expectations when it went on to become a critical and commercial success. It's tough to hang with it today, but at the time it represented a fresh perspective on the Simpsons in video games that had failed to gel with the public until its release. *The Simpsons Bowling* and *The Simpsons Wrestling* kicked things off with their focus on a larger cast of playable characters in a clunky package, and *The Simpsons Road Rage* was arguably the zenith of that design. But not satisfied with that, Fox Interactive decided the cast of the show could fit into another popular video game format: *Tony Hawk's Pro Skater.*

There were skateboarding video games before *Tony Hawk's Pro Skater* premiered in 1999, and there were other skateboarding games after it, but *THPS* set a particularly fun standard for the genre that led to big sales and a franchise that eventually burned itself out until the nostalgia-driven remasters announced just recently in 2020. The games featured real pro skaters at a time when X-treme sports athletes were the next wave of popular trend setters. More importantly, the games featured their real moves with a well-designed control scheme that allowed players to fly high in the air and cycle through any number of cool poses and tricks in order to watch the satisfying accrual of points in the corner. The maps were also more akin to skate parks than the downhill slaloms of such games in the nineties, and these open environments tagged along with the more prominent technical ambassadors such as *Grand Theft Auto III* to break away from corridor-based level design and allow players to simply roam around in big, decadent spaces.

So the template was there by the time Fox Interactive looked around to find someone to create a Simpsonized take on skateboarding. It's not clear if this was a case of the publisher seeking a developer, or if the developer pitched it to them à la Radical Entertainment's approach with *The Simpsons Road Rage*. Either way, the project led to another partnership between Electronic Arts and Fox Interactive, and a new developer in the mix: The Code Monkeys.

The Code Monkeys, like most of the development studios in this book, were a veteran of the game industry by the time the Simpsons kickflipped onto their doorstep. The studio was established in the late eighties by British programmers Colin Hogg, Mark Kirby, and Elliot Gay, and initially focused on games for largely European platforms such as the ZX Spectrum and Amiga line of computers. They pivoted to become a port house as console money swept through the nineties, with titles like *Turrican* for the Sega Genesis and *Universal Soldier*, a notable licensed game in their early catalog. The company trudged along into the PlayStation era and steadily took on more ports and licensed games across different genres, including the adventure in Disney's *Goofy's Fun House* and a mini game-driven treasure hunt in *Shrek: Treasure Hunt* just before they began their work on their one and only *Simpsons* game.

As noted above, the game was delayed numerous times throughout 2002 and never received the same level of advertising or marketing support as *The Simpsons Road Rage*, and indeed was only released for the PlayStation 2 instead of getting spread across multiple platforms. The game itself tells the tale as to why a company like Electronic Arts might choose to quietly complete its commitment and release the title. But Electronic arts wouldn't give up on skateboarding just yet, releasing the *skate.* series by their EA Black Box studio starting in 2007.

Even after that quiet release, The Code Monkeys persevered. They kept on with licensed games for several years, then took on budget projects for mobile and the burgeoning digital space on consoles such as Nintendo Wii and PlayStation 3. They even took a stab at self-publishing the *Triple Sports* series of games before deciding to shut down completely in early 2011. One might lament the end of any company as its employees must disperse and find new jobs, but a stretch of nearly thirty years is impressive. If only we could remember them for more than their longevity.

The mean streets of a Springfield diorama.

The gang's all here... again. As in *The Simpsons Wrestling* and *The Simpsons Road Rage*, this game's design focuses on throwing in a variety of playable characters from the television show and ensuring they have lots of dialogue to spew while they traverse their respective versions of Springfield. Players can choose from Homer, Bart, Marge, and Lisa, then unlock additional characters such as Nelson Muntz, Otto, Professor Frink, Krusty, and of course... Chief Wiggum? Was there a survey that determined Wiggum is a popular enough character to throw into a skateboarding game? In any case, the premise is even flimsier than *Road Rage* in that the player is once again vying for cash and points, but there is no villain except one's innate ability to perform skate tricks or fail spectacularly. The only goal is to win an oddly specific $99 prize. As the game manual states while presumably trying to excite the player to play the game, "We're talking literally dozens of dollars here!"

Motivation aside, this game is all about skateboarding. The *Tony Hawk's Pro Skater* series was in its fourth iteration by the time *The Simpsons Skateboarding* released, and it's safe to say the genre founded by that series laid out a neat little set of game design rules for savvy game developers to follow. Those basic rules are in place in this game as well, with players controlling their chosen skater from a third-person perspective and perpetually glued to their skateboard, left with no choice but to skate forward and eat asphalt in a Sisyphean cycle of skating terror. Each skater possesses their own set of strengths and weaknesses across five skill categories: Speed, Turns,

Jumps, Grabs, and Grinds. These categories determine each character's starting skills, but players can accrue money during a career playthrough that is then used to pump up the skill levels for each category. It is the game's only use for the weirdly miniscule amounts of money earned while skating (always in increments ranging from $0.10 to $0.50), but provides some motivation for sticking to a particular character and completing the game's challenges.

The game gets surprisingly technical in its implementation of skateboarding tricks and moves. Code Monkeys clearly did their homework in that respect and it makes me think that a better skateboarding game might have come out of this if the developers weren't tied to the *Simpsons* license. Instead, players have to watch clunky 3D models of *Simpsons* characters repeatedly perform tricks and moves that take time to properly learn and execute. With experience, players can learn to navigate vert ramps and pipes and pull off intricate strings of trick combos that allow the player to achieve temporary In the Zone boosts and amass higher and higher scores, and in turn unlock more of the game as they go. The challenge is there for hardcore skateboard players, but when they have Neversoft's far superior Tony Hawk series there's no reason to play this game. Conversely, the gameplay is too hardcore for casual fans of *The Simpsons* who are just interested in seeing their favorite characters tell jokes while exploring Springfield. It's a classic case of attempting to appease both worlds and satisfying neither.

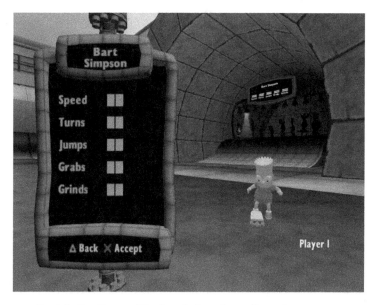

Bart is the Super Mario of skateboarding characters.

While the full assortment of grabs and slides and flips are all here, the game isn't content to simply allow the player to perform those tricks as the core gameplay experience, and with good reason. It gets kind of boring quite quickly in this application. The developers opted to include a mode they call Skate the Tour, which is the game's primary career mode and is the means by which players can unlock new skaters, maps, and money to upgrade said skaters. Each map unlocked in Skate the Tour mode comes along with three types of challenges. Timed Trick Contest is just as it describes, a mode in which players must perform tricks within a time limit. Skillz School serves as both a tutorial on learning new moves and a challenge in learning how to string those moves and tricks together to increase point yields. Finally, there's Skatefest, and this is where players will spend most of their time. They are free to roam the map and complete a variety of objectives that boil down to collecting things and achieving a certain score within a time limit. These objectives serve to guide the player around the map and ensure they get to see all the nooks and crannies of the sprawling maps, but they are quite the challenge to complete. I wouldn't be surprised if most players never got past Springfield Elementary, the first map in the game that features the school and a small collection of businesses and parks around it.

It may seem lonely to have to skate around a big map while collecting stuff, but the game provides a constant companion in the form of narration by Kent Brockman. The developers thankfully included the option to disable Kent Brockman's running commentary, which immediately collapses into a repetition of commentary about each trick performed instead of being idle observations about a player's performance, allowing an opportunity for, you know, jokes. I would've preferred to see color commentary à la the interstitial scenes in *Bart vs. the Juggernauts* (Chapter 8), but Harry Shearer's infamous curmudgeonry about lending his voices to other products probably limited the amount of dialogue the developers could include. The player skaters will also chime in with short remarks and exclamations, and other characters also wander the environments and drop lines of dialogue, but these dialogue lines are all few and far between. While there is also music for aural accompaniment, it all falls into that bizarre genre of music I'll call techno-ska that feels like it belongs in a skateboarding game from the nineties and not in a game based on a television show with renowned orchestral music by Alf Clausen.

This interrogation will end quickly if you cooperate.

As mentioned, the environments themselves are huge and it's cool to see familiar characters and landmarks, but it's quite awkward to explore those environments while riding an unstoppable skateboard. The maps are simply too much, creating huge and intimidating spaces to explore with just a skateboard to navigate them. The player can always pause in place and have a look around, but it's not the ideal way to tour Springfield. This drawback once again highlights the awkward mash-up of this license and the skateboarding gameplay. The huge environments might have been a plus in an open world action or adventure game, but not in a skateboarding game where the environments have to be relatively free of the kind of minutiae fans of *The Simpsons* would love to slow down and gawk at. There are certainly landmarks—hey, there's Springfield Elementary! And Krusty Burger!—but the space in between is filled with bland and featureless half pipes, rails, and vertical ramps, which are all well and good for a skatepark but stand out like a sore toe in the middle of Springfield locations that fans of the show know too well.

The game's finale level is the infamous Springfield Gorge from the "Bart the Daredevil" episode in season two. It is perhaps the show's prime moment in which skateboarding plays an important part in the story. It's certainly cool to have the opportunity to jump the gorge like Homer tried (and horribly failed) to do in the show, but it requires playing through nine other levels of varying appeal to unlock it. It once again makes me wonder what Code Monkeys could have done if this wasn't tied to a cartoon sitcom. Once the player unlocks all the maps and completes the challenges, there's really no reason to go back in. There's a multiplayer mode I suppose, but even that is lackluster and feels tacked on as a compromise in trying to match what the competitors were doing.

Bracing for the sudden and inevitable betrayal of gravity.

The game just floats in a limbo. It proves its technical chops with the intricate move and trick gameplay, not to mention the impressively huge maps right out of sprawling platformer epics of the era like *Jak and Daxter* or *Ratchet & Clank*. But it fails to create something that fans of the television show would want to explore, and its reliance on the license ruins its appeal for fans of the well-established skateboarding genre. The game floats between the two worlds as a half-formed entity, and its disappointing sales of only 160,000 units shows the idea just didn't click with customers. I wish I could say the idea had potential, but it just feels like it was doomed to fail from conception.

Notes

1. *Noiseland.co* (2021). Still kicking after all these years. Retrieved 21 March 2021.

Chapter 20: The Odds Against Them

The Simpsons Hit & Run - September 2003

Life trudged on in 2003. The endless war of our times intensified as the United States and its allies invaded Iraq and ended the decades-long regime of Saddam Hussein, the world was enraptured by the whirlwind romance of Bennifer, and Clay Aiken won the hearts of the nation even as he came in second place to Ruben Studdard on American Idol. *The Simpsons* was in its fifteenth season by the end of the year, while fellow Fox Television Network sitcoms such as *The Pitts*, *The Grubbs*, and soon-to-resurge *Family Guy* all fell by the wayside into the cancellation ditch.

Outside of the "Treehouse of Horror" episodes, I wasn't watching *The Simpsons* any longer. Like many fans, it wasn't a conscious choice to stop watching. Life was simply getting busier and busier, and *The Simpsons* no longer had the chops of the golden era in the nineties. It became the background noise, always on television on Sundays and guaranteed to appear multiple times a day in syndication. In spite of that, I remained strangely focused on documenting the video games derived from the license. I still wrote walkthroughs, and still updated my fansite. It was a nice bit of ritual activity as uncertainty swirled around. I was approaching the end of my time in college by 2003 and left to ponder where and how and who one is meant to become in adulthood. There was a vague notion of starting a career in video games, but there was no focal point to my vision. It wasn't until the end of the year when a shining yellow beacon would emerge to light the way.

Marge Simpson, patron saint of road rage.

The intense period of the *Simpsons* video game renaissance was nearing its crescendo. We'd seen five games in three years, and tremendous peaks and valleys in terms of the quality of those games. Before 2003, *The Simpsons Road Rage* was the unquestioned high point of the era, providing a fun gameplay experience while also featuring as many characters as they could cram in there and lots of one-liners. As evidenced by the aforementioned tremulous quality of many of the games released by a variety of publishers, *Road Rage*'s success was entirely driven by the dedication and craftsmanship of the team at Radical Entertainment in cooperation with Fox Interactive. It was enough of a critical and commercial success that Radical decided they would try for a second miracle.

Securing the rights to develop a game based on such a huge license may seem like a daunting task for anyone but the biggest of publishers, but Fox Interactive was in a different phase of its video game efforts and more willing to take a smaller cut. As Radical designer Joe McGinn put it, "as a small developer all we had to do was convince Fox that we had a great game concept and development team."[1] And while Fox Interactive was happy to work with Radical again on developing a game with the *Simpsons* license, they still weren't in a place to provide the necessary funding. That meant another go-round of pitching a new game to publishers after *Road Rage* had shipped. Electronic Arts seemed the odds-on favorite given their success with *Road Rage* and the fact that they were the publisher of the two most recent releases, but for some reason they opted to pass on their next project. Instead, a critical business restructuring laid the groundwork for the next game. Fox sold its video game arm—the entirety of Fox Interactive's assets—to Vivendi Universal Games, a mid-tier publisher known mostly for licensed titles such as *The Hobbit* and *Buffy the Vampire Slayer.*

Vivendi Universal Games itself was an entity derived from numerous mergers and renaming efforts, but the long and short of it is that Vivendi, the media conglomerate based in France, wanted to get into the video game space and decided to do so by buying another French company called Havas Interactive, which included ownership of a little developer called Blizzard Entertainment. All the mergers led to the 2003 formal foundation of Vivendi Universal Games as a subsidiary of the larger Vivendi empire. Fox Interactive joined them and brought along its licenses, including *The Simpsons.* This kind of shakeup could have had disastrous results for the *Simpsons* project that had then been in development for nearly two years, but fortunately all parties involved decided Radical's new game would be worth the investment. And oh boy, would those dividends ever pay off.

That aforementioned two year development period did not come easy. Typical console game development for Radical at the time was about twelve months, which in reality was too short a period to produce a high quality title. But Radical guaranteed themselves some extra time thanks to tricky schedule manipulation. Joe McGinn recalls, "I think our producer was quite clever here, arranging the game to be 'finished' in February ... knowing full well this would allow him to negotiate another six months of dev time and still hit Xmas."[2] In an interview with game archivist Liam Robertson, Radical tech director Vlad Ceraldi described how shocking it was to work with a publisher that was willing to invest in quality:

> You know, they were game to spend more money and more time, which was—it's rare. You don't often get those opportunities. We had very little time but the team was pretty enthusiastic about the additional time and how we could use it...[3]

The extra time gave Radical the wiggle room to craft a game that would far surpass their effort with *Road Rage*. They stuck with the basic formula of a driving game, but as *Simpsons* executive producer Matt Selman notes, "There was this huge argument over whether they could get out of the cars... and kick each other."[4] It was a challenge for a development team that had focused solely on driving mechanics to include character control, level design that took advantage of allowing characters to run around, and implementing open world levels in the style of *Grand Theft Auto*. But they worked through it, got the time they needed to figure it out, and they managed to ship the aptly titled *The Simpsons Hit & Run* for PlayStation 2, Xbox, Nintendo Gamecube, and Windows PCs by the fall of 2003. The game would go on to become the highest-rated *Simpsons* game in history and the biggest commercial success to date. Its success would remain unchallenged for the next several years as the release of

Simpsons games ceased and the license shifted to a new publisher.

As luck would have it, the Vivendi Universal Games office was based just fifteen minutes from the house where I grew up in Los Angeles, and the stars aligned enough to allow me to get a job there in 2004. Over time, I learned tidbits about the game's development and release. The most notable story I heard was that the success of *The Simpsons Hit & Run* allowed many employees of the publisher to remain employed, since other releases that year such as *The Hobbit* and *Metal Arms: Glitch in the System* had failed to achieve sales targets.

That little development studio called Blizzard Entertainment would go on to release a game called *World of Warcraft* a year later, which was the beginning of the end for Vivendi's game business. They bought Radical in 2006 to develop *Crash Bandicoot* games, and continued publishing a variety of original and licensed titles, but the success of *World of Warcraft* overshadowed all other game publishing efforts. Corporate hawks hungrily eyed Vivendi's profits from the MMORPG business, and it was ultimately Activision that swooped in and bought Vivendi's game business in late 2007. I was gone from Vivendi by then, pursuing that silliest of goals: to work on a *Simpsons* video game.

Mission: turn yourself in.

The elevator pitch for *The Simpsons Hit & Run* is that it's an open world mission-based video game featuring all the characters you love from *The Simpsons* and a mysterious plot involving robotic wasp cameras and aliens. It's interesting in the context of 2003 because it seems to fit with the paranoia of the times, in which the government has no qualms about abusing its power to spy on foreigners and citizens alike in pursuit of terrorist shadows. This is reflected in the game's early narrative. Mysterious black vans have invaded Springfield in connection to giant wasp-shaped cameras wandering around and illicitly recording Springfield citizens. If it all sounds too weird for something one might see on the television show, it's because the writers for the game finally realized they could craft a narrative on par with the show's writing without sacrificing the inherently bizarre nature of a video game.

Just like in those beloved "Treehouse of Horror" episodes, the developers could chuck the rules out the window and make up something fun and funny that wasn't too weird for players. Interestingly, the story we got in the final game isn't what was planned from the beginning. As part of his deep dive into the game's development, Liam Robertson discovered that there was originally quite a different story to move the player along. In his words, "Without warning, Gracie Films decided to revise the script partway into development, diverging from the initial storyboards Radical had prepared." This led to "many hours of work being scrapped," which was not an uncommon result of working with Gracie Films.[5] They only understood that it was their property and it needed to shine as brightly as possible. Great for players, bad for overworked developers.

Players were well-versed in open world sandboxes by 2003. *Grand Theft Auto III* shipped in 2001 and paved the way for a multitude of games fashioned as *GTA* clones, games in which a player was free to roam about in an environment without necessarily having to follow a prescribed narrative. There often was still a story to follow, as with *Hit & Run*, but players could also choose to completely ignore the missions in favor of goofing around by attacking wandering NPCs, driving vehicles up and down the boulevards, and trying to get into places they shouldn't be. This open-ended design heavily informed *Hit & Run*'s mission structure. While *Hit & Run* did still break up its story across seven levels, and thus wasn't as open a world as those in *Grand Theft Auto*, it allowed the team to feature different characters in each level and include more of Springfield than they could fit in a single map.

Out of the way, my favorite baseball squadron is playing on TV!

The game's levels consist of three core areas—the suburbs, downtown, and seaside docks—each of which is repurposed and tweaked to make up the game's seven levels. Each level then consists of seven story missions and a bonus mission to unlock a special vehicle. The playable character in each level also varies, moving along in sequence: Homer, Bart, Lisa, Marge, Apu, Bart again, and finally Homer again for the finale level in which the suburbs are reskinned to become a pastiche of the television show's "Treehouse of Horror" episodes. This particular level is a fan favorite, including yours truly. Even then, it wasn't guaranteed to make the cut. Game designer Joe McGinn noted, "The only reason it made it was because the team loved the idea so much, it was a real labor of love."[6] It was a final victory lap for the team, a chance to go all out with something fun and appropriate to the game's spooky *X-Files* vibe. The level design is bolstered by visuals that never quite match the quality of the television show but are fine for a 3D game of this era, and upbeat music that captures the more fast-paced driving missions that make up the majority of the game.

It's quite the journey to get to that final "Treehouse of Horror"-themed level. The game begins with the oddly repetitive opening scene from many of the video games: Homer on the couch, watching television. He decides to go out for snacks, and thus kicks off a series of twists and turns in which it is revealed that mysterious black vans and wasp-shaped drone cameras are spying on the good people of Springfield. The story turns into an investigation as each of the characters pursues their leads while racing and crashing their way around a fully populated Springfield. It's not the deepest story and in fact probably isn't the guiding force behind a player's desire to keep going, but it provides that important framework that so many other *Simpsons* games are lacking. It doesn't feel as flimsy as what we've experienced so far in *Simpsons* games, and in turn comes across as the game's designers and writers actually respecting the intelligence of their players. While *Simpsons* writers Matt Selman, Tim Long, and Matt Warburton were credited with story and dialogue for the game, McGinn revealed that it was actually game designer Chris Mitchell who took on the brunt of the work with the game's writing.[7] It's an impressive effort and undoubtedly a key element of the game's creative success.

Video game Homer is the most athletic Homer.

The game is necessarily light in its combat and economy design. Players can kick other characters and objects, and while objects are destructible, other characters simply fall and flail about until they regain

303

their composure and continue on their way. This sounds as strange as it is, but its execution is just so weird and fun that it is simply another brick in the wall that makes up this game's great achievement. As YouTuber minimme notes in his excellent review, "The bouncy, care-free, just-have-fun toy box approach is, to some extent, this game's lightning in a bottle moment."[8] It knows it's a video game, and while it's not as meta as later iterations on *Simpsons* video games, it's certainly a wink at the player. As minimme puts it, "It's a game that sacrifices long-term satisfaction for short-term joy."[9] These actions aren't completely without consequence. Players must collect coins as currency to purchase costumes and vehicles, but they must be careful not to increase their Hit & Run meter too much as they attack characters and destroy objects and vehicles. If the meter is filled, cops appear and give chase until the player outruns them or gets caught. The penalty for getting caught is a small amount of coins, but those coins become precious as the game goes on and missions require the player to purchase new costumes and vehicles to continue.

Vehicle gameplay is what Radical knew best when they began the project, and no one could have faulted them for taking what they had with *Road Rage* and transposing it to their new open world sandbox engine. Instead, Radical went back to the drawing board to reengineer the vehicle controls, physics, and even the fact that vehicles take damage and explode if they exceeded their damage limits, something they hadn't achieved in *Road Rage*. This fragility allowed them to not only tweak vehicle parameters such as speed and handling, but also vehicle health, a key element of the *Grand Theft Auto* games that makes world traversal that much more interesting. A vehicle that is damaged becomes a liability during missions, and a destroyed vehicle can only be repaired at a high cost. Players can find wrench power-ups throughout the levels that allow them to repair vehicles instantaneously, encouraging them to think strategically as they dart and weave through traffic on their way to the next target. Indeed, although some missions require the player to leave their car, most missions consist of a select few types of vehicle gameplay including races, smashing or evading other cars, and collecting objects from the road.

Apu, you hot tamale you.

These missions often lead the player around the level maps, ensuring every inch of the maps is revealed over time if a player chooses not to explore on their own. They are never very difficult until the last missions in the last couple of levels, and in particular the very final mission of the game in which Grampa Simpson's jet-powered Jeep must be driven to the site of an alien spaceship without bumping into anything lest the radioactive waste cargo gets jostled and blows up. One gets the sense that there was a design mandate to make these missions as difficult as possible for the sake of drawing out the final hours of the story. It's an erratic difficulty spike that many players of *Hit & Run* remember with a mixture of trepidation and disdain. It doesn't mar the experience, but caps it with a challenging mission and well-earned finale cutscene.

The Simpsons Hit & Run is now spoken of with the kind of awe usually reserved for classics such as the *Super Mario Bros.* or *Crash Bandicoot* series. Many fondly remember the game from their childhoods, and upon examination it's clear that Radical hit upon something entirely unique in the history of *Simpsons* games, both those that came before and the games released afterward. Somehow, despite pressure to hit the holiday sales period, the developers also included collectible gags and cards, multiple costumes for all playable characters, and even a multiplayer mode, a distraction that provided up to four players the option to race around in small tracks à la the classic *R.C. Pro-am* on NES. With all these features and content, the game found the elusive combination of writing, gameplay, and visuals that allowed them to integrate an animated sitcom into a video game in a way that highlights the best of each medium while avoiding the pitfalls we've seen to date.

Oh, Lord, protect this rocket car and all who drive within the rocket car.

Vivendi, in its infinite wisdom, also released that Windows PC version of the game in a time before Valve's Steam storefront made the platform a business necessity. This decision led to a thriving modder community around the PC version spearheaded by the efforts of modders at the Donut Team forums, which in turn has provided ample fodder for YouTubers itching to find that next great video subject.[10] The mod content has generated renewed fervor in the game and ensured that a new generation of players can discover this now-classic game, even if it's through wacky mods and videos on YouTube.

Sadly, Radical's time with the license ended here, and while Vivendi considered porting the games to platforms such as Nintendo Game Boy Advance and the Sony PlayStation Portable, those versions never came to fruition. Vivendi's sole outing with the license ended with this game in 2003, and it would be several years before someone else took up the torch.

Notes

1. Joe McGinn, "Hello From a Hit & Run Designer" (Donut Team, 2016). Retrieved 21 March 2021.
2. Joe McGinn, "Hit & Run Development Challenges" (Donut Team, 2016). Retrieved 21 March 2021.
3. Liam Robertson, "The Simpsons Hit & Run's Lost Sequel + Fun Facts - Game History Secrets," *DidYouKnowGaming* (YouTube, 2019). Retrieved 21 March 2021.
4. "The Simpsons: 30 Years of Video Games and Jokes About Video Games" (YouTube, 2019). Archived by gameslice on youtube.com. Retrieved 21 March 2021.
5. Liam Robertson.
6. Joe McGinn, "A Day in the Life: Radical Entertainment" (Donut Team, 2016). Retrieved 21 March 2021.
7. Joe McGinn, "Hit & Run Development Challenges."

8. "The Simpsons Hit & Run retrospective review | minimme" (YouTube, 2020).

9. Ibid.

10. "Donut Team" (2021). Retrieved 21 March 2021.

Chapter 21: The Plopper

The Simpsons Hit & Run pleased pretty much everyone, and while it wasn't a perfect game by any means, it was certainly the best game to feature the Simpsons in a long time. Upon its release, I felt certain that Vivendi had struck the kind of gold that ensured at least one more round of the same type of gameplay. Perhaps a sequel with a larger, unified map to achieve the kind of open world they'd attempted in the first game?[1] And certainly more types of vehicles, more characters, more locales. More, more, more. It was quite a time to be a fan of *Simpsons* games, dreaming of what may be.

I was so certain that they'd try again that I decided I had the opportunity to contribute. I had no work experience in video games, mind you, and my college education opened me up to that type of work but I hadn't exactly studied game design or programming. Instead, I felt confident that I could get a job as a game tester at Vivendi Universal Games when I graduated from college in early 2004, just a few months after the release of *The Simpsons Hit & Run*. I mean, their office was right down the street in Los Angeles. Surely I'd be an instant hire.

Now I'm not usually that confident in my pursuits, but every once in a while I get it into my head that it can and must be done. So I applied at various game companies just to hedge my bets, but eventually did get the call from Vivendi, and I was hired to start in May 2004. I worked in their game test department for a year, then in online marketing, always waiting and casually asking when that next *Simpsons* game would appear on our forecasts. I'm sure the odd looks I was getting were not of concern but of admiration for my dogged pursuit of dumb goals. The game seemed certain to warrant a sequel, but the company simply chose not to invest in any further *Simpsons* games. However, according to Liam Robertson's look back at *Hit & Run*, former members of the development team confirmed that a sequel was somewhere in the planning stages before being cancelled.[2] It wasn't until November 2005 that I discovered the truth: Vivendi had given up the license, and Electronic Arts returned to scoop it up and develop a *Simpsons* game at their Redwood Shores studio.[3] Well, that pretty much sealed my fate. I left my job and Los Angeles behind in 2007, applied at Electronic Arts, and once again I rearranged my whole life for the chance to work on a *Simpsons* game.

While I was getting ready to move to the San Francisco bay area, EA Mobile back in Los Angeles was busy. The *Simpsons* license wasn't just for a new big console game, but also for the right to develop games for the fast-growing mobile market.

Cue the Benny Hill tune.

Mobile phones were a firmly established aspect of our reality by 2007. They first became popular in the eighties as commercial cellular telephones appeared in the hands of Wall Street bankers and celebrities who didn't mind lugging those old brick-sized phones around with them. Eventually, these cellular phones shrunk and began to add additional features. The first phones to feature games in them released in the mid-nineties, and included ports of simple games such as *Tetris*, *Scramble*, and *Snake*, all of which could be programmed to play on the LCD screens available on the phones of the time.

Eventually, mobile phones evolved to become portable computers, with complete operating systems and more advanced features that extended the capabilities of the devices beyond just phone calls and text messages. These early feature phones, as they became known, were often programmed to run on the Java platform, and so the games that were released on them were also programmed using that coding language. By the early aughts, there were hundreds upon hundreds of games being released around the world, many of which rose and fell with the feature phone market. The games could only be so complex, given that feature phone interfaces generally consisted of the number keys and four to six additional buttons known as soft keys which were used to navigate the operating system. This interface limited game designers, and while games such as *Tetris* worked perfectly in that format, the kinds of character-based action games that console players were accustomed to playing were more difficult to achieve.

But that didn't stop anyone from trying. Every major publisher spun up their respective mobile divisions to capitalize on the burgeoning market, and that included EA Mobile. The division was based out of Los Angeles and formed in 2004, then later expanded after Electronic Arts purchased the smaller mobile game publisher called JAMDAT Mobile. EA Mobile didn't just deal in games, but also ringtones (another big source of revenue) and other mobile applications. It was in this atmosphere that Electronic Arts acquired the *Simpsons* license and embarked upon the first of several mobile games based on *The Simpsons*.

Lord of donut town.

While EA Mobile was expanding, they didn't have all the development resources they needed to develop the games in their portfolio. Just as before, the publisher looked around for a developer to take on the task, and in this case EA Mobile struck the deal with a company called G5 Mobile. This prolific developer based out of Stockholm, Sweden goes as far back as the beginnings of the mobile market itself, having been founded in Russia in 2001 to develop for mobile and PCs. They struck gold with games like *Fight Hard 3D* and hitched their wagon to the license train, developing games based on *Pirates of the Caribbean*, *Scarface*, and *Star Wars* franchises. They were soon working with all the major publishers in the game industry, and that was when they signed the deal to work with EA Mobile in 2006.

The result of this collaboration was *The Simpsons Minutes to Meltdown*, a game scheduled to release along with *The Simpsons Movie* and all of its ancillary marketing madness in the summer of 2007. It wasn't a direct adaptation of the movie, but its own original work, though it did feature the bizarrely popular Plopper the Pig character that was introduced in the movie. I still remember the day that the movie was released. I stopped by one of many 7–11 convenience stores that had been rebranded as Kwik-E-Marts in a cool bit of capitalistic cross-promotion. I picked up a Squishee (the game's take on the Icee) and then proceeded to the movie theater where I arrived before the showtime, so I flipped open my Motorola Razr feature phone to play some *Minutes to Meltdown* before the movie began. You might think this is peak nerdy fandom, but friend, there were levels of nerdom ahead that I could not even imagine.

One should not be legally responsible for actions of popular pigs.

With the limitations of the feature phone hardware in mind, what did G5 Mobile accomplish? For starters, they were smart in limiting the design of the game to match the hardware. *Minutes to Meltdown* plays as an adventure game viewed from an isometric perspective, and the player's only real interactions are to use the arrow keys to move up, down, left, and right, and to use the action key to interact with elements in the environment. This is not unlike the point-and-click adventures popularized on PCs in the nineties. Homer is the only playable character and his goal is simple: stop the nuclear annihilation that his beloved Plopper has caused. In an interesting twist geared to the format, the game includes a hard thirty minute time limit to progress through the game's levels and stop the nuclear meltdown. Mobile phones then, just as now, were often best for playing in short bursts during lunch breaks, rides on buses and trains, or just when someone needed to kill a few minutes. By limiting the game's progression to just thirty minutes, the game encourages the player to see it through in a short session.

It's a light premise for a decidedly light-hearted license. It's enough to get the player into the game and exploring the world of Springfield as presented on a tiny screen with isometric pixel art. But it's a pretty game for what it is. Homer begins in the Simpson house, eager to find his car keys so he can drive to the Springfield Nuclear Power Plant and avert disaster. The house is perfectly laid out, and all of the spaces familiar to fans can be explored, such as the living room, the kitchen, and even the rooms on the second floor. Other Springfield characters also appear and present little moments for fans to discover by standing near them and pressing the action button when the OK prompt appears. There is little actual dialogue text, and instead Homer will see thought bubbles appear over characters' heads as clues to what he should do next. The NPC characters are also unfortunately rather stiff, and outside of enemies that run around, there isn't much animation to them. It's not the joke machine gameplay we saw from previous games, or from any episode of the show, but it works for the format.

Homer's got the shinning.

While Homer can explore and solve simple puzzles to unlock doors and progress further, there are still obstacles. Cops appear often and rather than seek to arrest Homer, they're all out to beat him senseless. Er, touch him senseless, relying on the tried and true formula of touching equals damage. Homer's health bar depletes through these interactions and the player must avoid or block enemies in order to evade their attacks, but there are also health pick-ups such as donuts and soda cans to replenish health.

The first level is simply the Simpson house, and serves as the game's introduction. The next level takes place on the streets of Springfield and that is where things really open up. It's still a highly linear game, mind you, but the level is much longer and feels bigger just by virtue of making the player traverse several city blocks and encounter plenty of familiar locales and characters along the way. That includes a run-in with Barney the coffee fiend (a reference to his controversial sobering up in "Days of Wine and D'oh'ses" from season eleven) and a crazed Krusty the clown tossing pies from the roof of a car. There are more simple puzzles required to unblock the path, and navigating hazards such as fires and moving cars. The game also introduces brief skateboard sections that amount to simple maneuvering around obstacles. Again, simple but pretty at such a low resolution. Their artists did good work.

Damn right, bring down all the statues.

The final level is the Springfield Nuclear Power Plant itself, and much like before consists of exploring the plant and solving simple lock-and-key puzzles to proceed to the next goal. As always, Homer is chasing down Plopper and avoiding enemies. This level's goons consist of power plant technicians in full radioactive garb, indicating that perhaps it's not safe to be there? Homer rolls on like the cartoon tank that he is. There are some fun bits with Homer clones assisting in solving puzzles, encounters with fan favorites Frink, Smithers, and Mr. Burns, and even a chopped arm as an inventory item. It's a goofy little finale for a game meant to be experienced in the span of a lunch break. The consequence of this is it is also quite forgettable, and while an interesting experiment, the game doesn't really do anything that sticks with the player after they finish it. Its most notable accomplishment is kicking off the series of games that would appear exclusively on mobile devices. No one knew it then, but mobile would become the final resting place of *Simpsons* video games.

Notes

1. "The Simpsons Hit & Run - Fully Connected Map Mod," *Colou* (YouTube, 2020). The first mod to allow players to drive around a map that fully connects the game's distinct areas. Retrieved 21 March 2021.

2. Liam Robertson, "The Simpsons Hit & Run's Lost Sequel + Fun Facts - Game History Secrets," *DidYouKnowGaming* (YouTube, 2019). Retrieved 21 March 2021.

3. Brendan Sinclair, "EA secures exclusive Simpsons license" (GameSpot, 2005). Archived by Internet Archive on web.archive.org. Retrieved 21 March 2021.

Chapter 22: The Swing for the Fences

The Simpsons Game – October 2007

I'd unwittingly stumbled into a fandom when I started watching *The Simpsons* on television, recorded episodes onto VHS tapes, and then found my own particular niche in the form of writing walkthroughs for *Simpsons* video games and creating a fansite to host those walkthroughs. Somehow, that wasn't enough, and I got it into my head that I needed to work on a *Simpsons* video game. I'd already grown up in Inglewood, California, a suburb just a stone's throw from Big Hollywood and all the video game and television production jobs I'd ever want. And while my stint at Vivendi Games was my foot in the door for video game work, it wasn't quite what I'd hoped. After all, I didn't just want to work on any video games. It had to be a *Simpsons* video game.

I was so determined that I left my job at Vivendi Games as soon as I discovered that the *Simpsons* license had landed at Electronic Arts. They were a multinational entertainment corporation by 2007, so it was helpful to see that EA specified they'd be working on a *Simpsons* video game at their EA Redwood Shores studio, just a six hour drive from Los Angeles and a more than manageable move. I applied through the normal channels on their website, and a friend of a friend even offered to place my résumé at the top of the pile. I'm ambivalent about that kind of nepotism now, but boy, it sure is important with a goal as specific as this.

Trouble was I left my job in February, and then it was just... silence. I stayed with my folks while my fate hung in the balance, and I even applied at other video game companies and for every position I could find. Marketing, production, testing; it all felt like a good fit, and I would have taken any job that gave me the opportunity to contribute to a *Simpsons* game in any appreciable fashion. I hung around in Inglewood for a couple of months, then rode through the California desert in a car with no name, until finally, miraculously, I got the call. EA were ramping up for their annual tester rush as they finalized games over the summer to sell in the fall. It required me to be in the San Francisco bay area for the interview, but after all the road tripping I'd done it was no thing to drive up again.

Long story long, I interviewed and got the job—I was a tester at Electronic Arts. My elation knew no bounds. Though they placed me on a *Sims* game at first, I had the audacity to tell my manager—as a tester not more than two weeks on the job—that I was actually there to work on *The Simpsons Game*. The gambit worked and I was finally plopped in front of an early build in June 2007. I ended up on the small team working on the PlayStation Portable version of the game, which was the most technically compromised version, but I didn't care.[1] It was four glorious months of a dream fulfilled. I hid my status as a *Simpsons* fansite nerd just in case it was a conflict of interest, but their marketing team reached out to me via the fansite and actually found out I worked on the game itself. Thankfully they just thought it was cool that a mega fan was working on the game, and they invited me to come along for the actual release party of *The Simpsons Game* down at the Hard Rock Cafe in Hollywood.[2] It was a long night of much booze, and ended with a small group of us fansite nerds getting a photograph with the man himself, Matt Groening. It was a surreal experience that capped off an unbelievable series of fortunate events.

You, too, can chase your nerdy dreams!

But I skipped to the end here, so let's see what was going on before drunken photos with cartoonists.

Electronic Arts was back, baby, and they brought their deep pockets with them. Having briefly lost the license to Vivendi Games, they came back around with what is inarguably the biggest and most ambitious *Simpsons* video game ever made. The company had the dough to not only invest in the license, but also the production and development of a game full of new patented technology for the next generation of hardware—Xbox 360 and PlayStation 3. This seventh generation of hardware represented the pinnacle of technical excellence in home consoles.

The team selected to design and develop a new *Simpsons* game for the latest generation was EA Redwood Shores. This development team was formed in 1998 alongside its parent company's new headquarters in—you guessed it—Redwood Shores, a suburb of the larger Redwood City area in the middle of San Francisco's peninsula. Before *TSG*, the EARS team were known for developing sports games such as the *Tiger Woods* series, as well as licensed action titles from the *Lord of the Rings*, *James Bond*, and *Godfather* licenses. Those games weren't known as great action titles, but they were serviceable vehicles for telling stories in those universes. It was *James Bond 007: From Russia With Love* that formed the technological backbone for many of their action games after 2005, and that included their new *Simpsons* game. They landed upon the idea of another action title in which the characters from *The Simpsons* television show would discover that they are actually in a video game, and use that to explore the series's history in video games and just make fun of video game tropes at every available opportunity. The story was penned by writers of the show, representing the closest collaboration yet between Gracie Films as the production company of the show and their video game counterparts. This collaboration was meant to bring about the definitive *Simpsons* video game experience. As one developer noted in the cancelled commentary, "I'm really happy and proud to have finally been on the product that's going to say that this is the *Simpsons* game, the [one] that everyone's been waiting for."[3]

Leaping into the advertising abyss.

I only joined near the end as a tester in summer 2007, so it's not clear exactly when they kicked things off. A prototype shared on YouTube by Morgan Kuno indicates that a team from EA had the game running in the *James Bond* engine as early as 2004, and given that the prototype was on the original Xbox, it is likely that it was a prototype used to convince Fox of their intentions with the new game.[4] By the time of the game's announcement in late 2006, EA was well underway and closing in on the release of the game about a year later.

Most of the resources were dedicated to fleshing out the premiere versions of the game on Xbox 360 and PlayStation 3, but EA was no fool in the face of dollars, and they made sure to also develop versions of the game for Nintendo's Wii, the portable platforms PlayStation Portable and Nintendo DS, as well as one more dip into the previous generation of platforms with the PlayStation 2. EA Redwood Shores was big, but only so big, and so they strictly handled development of the Xbox 360 and PlayStation 3 versions of the game, contracting all the others to Rebellion Developments for what was known as "current gen" (PlayStation 2, PlayStation Portable, Nintendo Wii) and Amaze Entertainment for Nintendo DS. Both companies were well-established as port houses that took on these sorts of projects, and while they both faced tough challenges in translating the game to platforms with less capable hardware, they still managed some impressive work in fitting the game to the limitations.

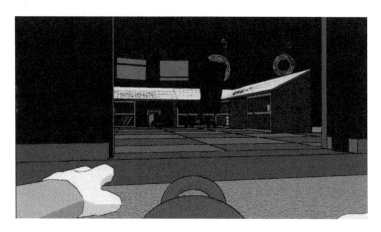

First-person crawling is due for a comeback.

EARS seemed intent on surpassing *Hit & Run* in every conceivable way, perhaps understanding that game's lasting place in the minds of gamers and the need to provide a new and improved experience in order to make a big splash. The game levels have hints of an attempt to replicate what worked about *Hit & Run*, especially in the game's recreation of the Springfield suburbs and the downtown area, but this element comes up quite short in comparison. The world feels relatively empty, populated by passersby who quote their lines from the television show but nothing relevant to the player's objectives. Still, as the cancelled developer commentary reveals, it was quite the effort:

> That was a big challenge, a lot of animations, every character is different, I mean this is one game I've worked on... it's phenomenal... we've got I think over 140 in game characters from the show. I think

total you'll see about 200, but everyone is unique, everyone got a different high and [they're] true to the model sheets.[5]

As the game progresses, the open world changes slightly, with new characters and interactions popping up. Overall, however, it serves as a hub between levels that's a bit too big for its britches. This open world Springfield is actually removed from the Rebellion and Amaze versions of the game, and while it may seem like a player is getting less game because of it, I'd say it is a vast improvement. If the open world can't achieve what *Hit & Run* did, why bother?

Fortunately—or perhaps unfortunately for players who miss *Hit & Run*'s open nature—the majority of the game takes place through a sequence of bespoke levels that each feature a different member of the Simpson family. According to one of the developers in the cancelled commentary:

> We have 16 unique levels. Unlike a lot of other games, we actually don't reuse a lot of game ideas between each level. Each level is pretty unique, and each level kind of stands alone as a really, really good game in itself.[6]

Each level also features a key player with a second character there for support and to provide another character for co-op gameplay. This dynamic of two characters pairing up to tackle various challenges provides welcome changes to the dialogue and gameplay in each level, and allows all of the family to get some time in the spotlight, something that we have seen prioritized since the second wave of *Simpsons* games kicked off in 2000.

Marge's innate ability to rally a mob pays off.

As noted before, the story was actually penned by writers from the television show this time, and it shows in the game's many cutscenes, dialogue regularly spouted by characters, and even the game's overall three-act structure. The majority of those pre-rendered cutscenes actually feature 2D animation on par with that of the show. This wasn't always the case—the cutscenes were all originally rendered using the in-game character assets, but someone at Gracie Films or Fox decided they'd pony up the cash to replace them with animation that admittedly looked far better than what could be accomplished with the 3D assets. This resulted in a near-total replacement of all the cutscenes in the game at a fairly late stage, throwing out work that EA's animators had labored over and requiring us testers to go back and replay every version of every game to make sure the cutscenes were okay. Gracie Films had struck again, but the result is several episodes' worth of original animation, and if nothing else, a pretty good reason to go back to explore the game. And for those curious to see the old cutscenes, they still shipped with the Nintendo DS version of the game.[7]

The gameplay of the levels in that three-act structure is perhaps the most maligned aspect of the game. It's understandable—while cutscenes and dialogue are all great, and there are some fun design ideas in the game's levels, many of them can feel like a slog to get through. The early levels in which the characters discover their abilities feel like a reasonable pace. Homer masters his ability to turn into a human rolling boulder, Bart tries out his Bartman abilities such as a grappling hook in the sewers, Lisa's power of meditation manifests as a god hand that can move objects around a logger's camp, and Marge's power of nagging allows her to control mobs and direct them to topple City Hall.

As the game progresses, each character unlocks upgrades and abilities that play on their base set of skills. Homer can become a giant fireball when he consumes an insanity pepper, a huge gummi blob with ranged attacks when he eats a gummi venus candy, and even a briefly lightweight balloon that can float about in the air. Bart's powers as Bartman allow him to glide for long distances and shoot more powerful ammo from his slingshot, and he also gets the ability to turn into an armored robot with laser attacks. Lisa's saxophone attack is upgraded with the ability to confuse enemies so they attack each other; her Hand of Buddha power improves to allow her to electrocute, burn, and freeze them all; and just for good measure, she has the ability to briefly take on her superpowered alter-ego, Clobber Girl. Finally, there's Marge, and while she doesn't get as much as the others in the cast, she still gets to improve her megaphone's range and its power to command minions from greater distances, in addition to a temporary Cop Marge power to, uh... be a cop. These simple upgrade tracks aren't particularly necessary as the difficulty is never that far beyond the base abilities, but levels are designed to accommodate those upgrades and give the player some extra stuff to do in the latter parts of the game.

A visit to the revisionist history museum.

Upon discovering their abilities, the town is invaded by those familiar tentacled aliens, Kang and Kodos. This leads to the game's slow middle section, in which the characters must again use their abilities to best a series of platforming and boss challenges. Progressing through these areas slows the game down considerably and the sometimes confusing level design only hinders the player's efforts. The final arc of the game gets the characters back to the fun with parodies of RPGs, war shooters, and even a metaphysical search for their own creator. My personal favorite levels are in this part of the game where the self-referential humor of the show shines through.

In hindsight, however, it generally feels like a marriage of television and game design that just didn't work out as well as one could have hoped. Matt Selman, executive producer and writer on the television show, contributed to the game, and has noted his surprise that it isn't as highly regarded as *The Simpsons Hit & Run*.[8] One of the developers in the cancelled commentary spoke to the challenge of integrating the show's humor into a video game:

> They tell you the jokes, its [sic] all based on timing, and then to get that crazy *Simpsons* wackiness and humor into the game, where its [sic] a user experience... It isn't completely timed for them, you don't know where the player's going to go, where they're going to wander in the environment, and to make sure that level of humor

stays true to the show has been a fun and interesting challenge too.[9]

I agree that the writing was excellent and Selman and his team should be proud of their work on the game, but it's not just another episode of the television show. A video game must live or die on the strength of its game design, and the gameplay of *The Simpsons Game* unfortunately has the tendency to stumble.

Lisa's sax whacks back, jack.

Players who could plod through the gameplay were rewarded with an embarrassment of joke riches. The idea was to feature as much dialogue and jokes as they could cram in there, along with cel-shaded graphics that were a vast improvement over the visuals of the previous takes on 3D video game characters. Between the writing and improved visuals, it was the closest players could get to playing in an episode of the show. And it wasn't just the usual cast of characters. The aforementioned Kang and

Kodos appear to bring the woo-woo Halloween vibe to the game, and even Sideshow Bob and God make appearances as the bosses for the game's central and final arcs, respectively. Not content to stop there, EA went for the flex by even including famed game designer Will Wright as the boss of the Game Engine section of the game, wherein Wright quips "I'm Will Wright, bitch!"[10]

As previously mentioned, several versions of the game were created to fit onto platforms that couldn't handle the requirements of the original "next gen" versions. Rebellion's ports for PS2, PSP, and Wii all shared the same codebase, built upon their proprietary Asura engine, and each had differences suited to their particular platform. The PS2 version was mostly the same except for lower resolution art and the removal of a few of the game's maps, and PSP was just a pared down version crammed onto the tiny screen. It was Nintendo's platforms that really shined in the porting process. The Wii version featured several mini games that were suited for the Wiimote controls, and the Nintendo DS port from Amaze was an entirely different game. It featured side-scrolling platforming and gameplay à la games from the NES and SNES eras, and utilized the stylus mechanic to include a Pet Homer mode in which players could poke and prod at their own lazy Homer digital pet.

Were you gonna eat that?

The game's journey culminates as a philosophical exploration in which the Simpson family struggles to understand what it means to be in a video game. Their quest mirrors the video game series's long struggle to find a place on the shelves of many players' collections, and although this was by far the most expensive and ambitious effort to date, it fell flat in some areas that players could never forgive. I'll say don't throw out the baby with the bathwater. EA made a game that addressed many of the concerns I've expressed over the course of this retrospective. They brought in the writers of the show and amped up the jokes to eleven, creating a satisfying and funny game that still stands out among the bleak and washed out tones of most action games of the era. Comedy in games is still not the norm, and while there are a few more *Simpsons* games to come, none of them quite measure up to this grand effort.

Notes

1. "PSP Testing for Dummies, by Dummies," (Noiseland.co, 2020). Retrieved 21 March 2021.
2. "The Simpsons Game Launch Party," (Noiseland.co, 2007). Retrieved 21 March 2021.
3. "The Simpsons Game (PlayStation 3, Xbox 360)" (The Cutting Room Floor, 2021). Retrieved 21 March 2021.
4. "The Simpsons Game March 8th 2004 Prototype, Original Xbox," *Morgan Kuno* (YouTube, 2019). Retrieved 21 March 2021.
5. "The Simpsons Game (PlayStation 3, Xbox 360)."
6. Ibid.
7. "The Simpsons Game (DS) Playthrough - NintendoComplete," *NintendoComplete* (YouTube, 2018). Retrieved 21 March 2021.
8. "The Simpsons: 30 Years of Video Games and Jokes About Video Games" (YouTube, 2019). Archived by gameslice on youtube.com. Retrieved 21 March 2021.
9. "The Simpsons Game (PlayStation 3, Xbox 360)."
10. "Will Wright," *Simpsons Wiki* (Fandom, 2021). Retrieved 23 March 2021.

Chapter 23: The Murder Park

The Simpsons Itchy & Scratchy Land - December 2008

The year of *The Simpsons Game* was the whirlwind it appeared to be in previous chapters. There was the movie, the first mobile game, *The Simpsons Game* itself, meeting Matt Groening at the launch party, and all of the crazy luck that went into getting myself involved in my own small way. It was such a whirlwind that by the end, I was kind of... done. Just done with caring about *The Simpsons*. My last bit of work as a tester on the game ended in October and I moved onto other, non-*Simpsons* projects at EA. In hindsight, that winter was kind of a bummer, and part of it was the fact that there was no way to match the dizzying highs of the first part of the year. But I hopped back on enough of the wagon to complete a walkthrough for *The Simpsons Game* in early 2008 because, hey, that's what I did back then.

In fact, writing walkthroughs was about the only thing that kept me coming back to games based on *The Simpsons* for the next decade. The company hosting my fansite shut down shortly thereafter and I just couldn't muster the motivation to host it again elsewhere, so all the work went straight to GameFAQs. I took a fairly long break as I recall, but I was back at the walkthrough writing game by 2013,

and I found a few new *Simpsons* games waiting for me
when I returned.

Running through a minefield, a smart and very good
decision.

EA never again attempted something on such a grand
scale as their 2007 end-all-be-all for *Simpsons* video
games. Their EA Redwood Shores studio shifted focus to
the *Dead Space* horror series and rechristened itself as the
edgy skull studio, Visceral Games. No other internal studio
bothered with *The Simpsons* again. It might've been the
middling reception to *The Simpsons Game*, or the relatively
high ROI (return on investment) in developing smaller
games with low-fi art and gameplay. In either case, they

still held onto the license and shifted their focus to the fast-growing mobile market.

EA Mobile followed up 2007's *Minutes to Meltdown* with a game cut from exactly the same cloth, and by the same developer. G5 Entertainment was still on the rise in the mobile space, and while the first iPhone debuted in 2007, the smartphone app market didn't exist yet. So they stuck with what they knew and developed another mobile game for Java and Blackberry feature phones. It was one last cheaply developed hurrah before the inevitable rise of the smartphone app.

The sage wisdom of the tutorial elder.

The Simpsons Itchy & Scratchy Land was not an innovative title when it was released in late 2008. The style was exactly what players had seen before in *Minutes to Meltdown* and other mobile games: isometric view, pixel graphics, and a playable character who could be moved around on an invisible grid by using the phone's keys to guide him along. Like *Minutes to Meltdown*, *Itchy & Scratchy Land* plays as a simple adventure game in which players progress to the next junction in a level to solve a small puzzle.

However, this more-or-less sequel to the first mobile game (which is actually called "The Simpsons 2" in the filename) did introduce some new mechanics and changes that showed G5 was willing and able to expand on the formula. For starters, *The Simpsons* television show was smack in the middle of their twentieth season when EA Mobile released *Itchy & Scratchy Land* in late 2008. While the video games so far had explored many different facets of the television series, one glaring omission was the renowned "Itchy & Scratchy Land" episode from season six in 1994. Sure, it appeared as a setting in mind-numbingly bland games like *The Simpsons Skateboarding*, but no other game had even bothered to play around in that space. The episode saw the family travel to the Itchy & Scratchy Land theme park and introduced myriad opportunities for the writers and animators to lampoon every aspect of the corporate theme park experience. While Disneyland was the easiest target, they also took cues from science gone amok movies like *Jurassic Park* and *Westworld* to take the typical bad theme park experience to its comedic extreme. This provided a rich backdrop for a video game, and while this mobile game wasn't quite the best way to explore such a wild episode, it did provide some more interesting and varied material for the developers to mine.

Saving Springfieldians from their own theme park avarice.

The most notable and easy way to leverage that episode's designs was to create themed levels that match the themed areas in the episode: Explosion Land, Unnecessary Surgery Land, Torture Land, and Searing Gas Pain Land. Each level's theme is represented in the environment art, such as the crater-ridden mine fields of Explosion Land or blood-splattered hospital beds of Unnecessary Surgery Land. Enemies also appear to swipe at the player. They include Itchy & Scratchy robots, giant axes, and other such recreations of the maniacal robots that appear in the episode. The theme park's central plaza serves as a hub between levels, as well as a trophy case in which other Springfield characters that are rescued during the course of levels will hang out. These characters don't have anything to say nor do they animate. In effect, they're creepy statues of characters you know, like Cletus and Mr. Burns. They are mere collectibles to "rescue" from the theme park attractions, however it does provide more reason to return to the various levels in the game, with rescued citizens tracked as part of the game's built-in achievements tracker. While each level does have its own distinct theme, the gameplay is copy-pasted between them, sometimes with reskins to apply some level of variation to what the player sees from one to the next.

Homer brave and true.

The Simpson family naturally has a more prominent role in the course of events, although like the last game, the playable character is all Homer all the way. He returns to serve as a kind of conveyance between puzzles, which are dumbed down to serve as little more than traversal puzzles, versus the lock-and-key puzzles of *Minutes to Meltdown*. Beyond navigating minefields and other hazards, Homer also has a bowling ball mini game in which the player must guide a rolling ball through a field of enemies and obstacles to unlock a gate at the other side. The other Simpson family members all feature only as mini game mechanics (except for Maggie, who is written out of the game just as she was in the episode by being dumped in a ball pit). Bart wields a slingshot and shoots at enemies after being guided by the player's reticle aiming, and Lisa appears to drop bombs in a similar mini game involving an aiming reticle. As a throwback to *The Simpsons* arcade game, Marge's weapon is a vacuum cleaner, and her gameplay varies a bit by requiring the player to suck up ammunition and then fire it at enemies. Her shots also ricochet, adding a layer of strategy that is missing from the other mini games.

Bart graces the scene with his crackshot slingshot skills.

The conclusion of the game takes the player back to the theme park central plaza to actually recreate the scene in the episode where the Simpsons use the flash on their cameras to discombobulate the robots. It's a nifty finale, but it's kind of arduous to get there. The game isn't nearly as short as the thirty minutes of *Minutes to Meltdown*, but the harsh damage caused by obstacles and the repetition of puzzles to extend the playtime isn't really all that interesting. The obstacles become more difficult, and there's even a medal system in which players can earn bronze, silver, and gold medals that are tracked as part of the game's meta achievements, but it ultimately comes down to how hardcore a mobile player someone was in 2008. It might have been a good way to kill time during a few commutes but it's tough to go back to it now. This game, like *Minutes to Meltdown*, is easy to find online and emulate in any number of Java app emulators, so it's thankfully fully available for the curious to check out. It's a bit of history to look up in the waning days of *Simpsons* video games.

Notes

1. "PSP Testing for Dummies, by Dummies," (Noiseland.co, 2020). Retrieved 21 March 2021.
2. "The Simpsons Game Launch Party," (Noiseland.co, 2007). Retrieved 21 March 2021.

Chapter 24: The Impostor

The Simpsons Arcade – December 2009

I imagine most people don't note the coming and going of games from digital distribution fronts. If a game appears on Steam or the App Store today, and then it disappears two years from now, it'll go mostly unnoticed. Such is the ephemeral nature of digital entertainment. It is hosted by someone, generally on behalf of a publisher, and then it disappears when said publisher no longer has the rights to sell it or is unwilling to spend money to update the game when an OS update breaks it.

But there are a few people who will notice. Sometimes a lot of people. In fact, some games gain more notoriety for the fact that they've been delisted from a digital store than from their initial release. *Scott Pilgrim vs. the World: The Game* is a fine example, having released in 2010 and then delisted in 2014, followed by six years of fan complaints and pleading until publisher Ubisoft finally brought the game back to modern platforms at the end of 2020.

Games based on *The Simpsons* aren't generally available on digital storefronts, but few of them garner the kind of intense fan following that prompts a publisher to spend the money to bring it back. Konami's *The Simpsons* arcade game (Chapter 1) was, of course, finally brought to consoles via XBLA and PSN in 2012 just to be delisted less than two years later. Those who purchased it can still download it onto their Xbox 360 or PS3, but it is just gone otherwise. Sites like Delisted Games and YouTube videos help to archive the existence of such games after they've disappeared, but it's always just a challenge to simply play the games as they were released.

And then there's that other *The Simpsons Arcade* game. It's lesser known than its progenitor but still generates some interest by the fans who remember playing it on their parents' iPhone or iPad.

Classic meet-cute.

The smartphone was well underway by 2009, but not so far away that the feature phone was dead. It was a classic transition period in which the old hardware is still readily available around the world even as new, sleek hardware makes its way into the pockets and bags of those who can afford the latest and greatest. For game publishers and developers, it can be a challenge to know when to cut off support for older hardware, but it wasn't quite the time. After all, more ports on more platforms means more money.

And so the folks at EA Mobile continued their publishing shenanigans on both feature phones and the new iPhone hotness after the previous release of *The Simpsons Itchy & Scratchy Land* in 2008. The iPhone 3GS had just been released and EA was raring to go with a new game that utilized the touch input of smartphones while still supporting the button-based controls of Java and Blackberry feature phones.

Their developer this time around was a newbie to *Simpsons* games and a relatively new member of the game development community as well. IronMonkey Studios, based in Melbourne, Australia, focused entirely on mobile game development since they began in 2008, and worked with publishers such as Jamdat, which became EA Mobile, and so the marriage of IronMonkey Studios and EA Mobile was inevitable. Their first games with EA Mobile were mobile ports of *Need for Speed: Undercover* and *The Sims 3*, major franchises that they managed to successfully translate to mobile phones.

I especially hate clowns but I *especially* hate suits.

The company was a shoe-in to take on the next *Simpsons* game from EA. In a cheeky bit of marketing, they decided to create a game they knew would generate nostalgic interest. After all, if fans are clamoring for *The Simpsons* arcade game, why not give it to them? Sure, it's not *The Simpsons Arcade* that Konami would release to XBLA and PSN in a few years, but I suppose they figured that any ol' *Simpsons* arcade game would do.

IronMonkey's star was on the rise and it was only a year later that they were absorbed into EA Mobile to become a first-party studio. They merged with another local developer, Firemint, to become Firemonkey Studios in 2012, and they still make mobile games to this day.

The studio's first at bat with the *Simpsons* license was an interesting experiment in expanding the production values to make use of the increased memory and graphic capabilities of the iPhone, while also making something bite-sized enough for people to want to play on the go. After all, the original *Simpsons Arcade* could be completed in under an hour, which feels just about right for a quick game session or two during a commute. The beat 'em up is also a fine genre for just tapping away to beat up bad guys. It was a good start toward something fun and worth playing.

The premise is about as dinky as the original beat 'em up game, albeit way more dumb. In the original game, the Simpsons all banded together to allow four players to go out in pursuit of Maggie, who's been kidnapped by Mr. Burns after she replaced her pacifier with his stolen diamond. This time, Springfield's version of the Illuminati have come together to hide some kind of secret plot to "steal all of Springfield's... uh, I don't know, natural resources or something" on a USB thumb drive, which Smithers then hides in a donut. He steps out into an alleyway and bumps into Homer before running away with the donut. Homer's stomach leads the way as he fights his way through the subsequent levels in pursuit of that donut. The plight of the common man, you know.

Just because it looks like Konami's Simpsons Arcade doesn't make it Konami's Simpsons Arcade!

Unlike the original game, this mobile take on *The Simpsons Arcade* omits multiplayer and includes no playable characters other than Homer. It seems like an odd choice now, but the state of the App Store and online mobile gaming in general was still in its infancy in 2009, so it may have been a technical challenge the publisher was unwilling to tackle with the budget they had. So it becomes a single player romp in which Homer's fisticuffs are the primary means of interaction with the world. He has additional abilities, such as a ground stomp that stuns enemies and a headbutt charge, but it's all fairly restricted to Homer's abilities as an overweight angry guy.

The recipients of said fisticuffs are a new and wide-ranging variant of the besuited thugs that attack players in the original game. This game, however, does a far better job of not just having variety in the appearance of the thugs, but in their abilities as well. The base thugs only punch Homer, but new and more challenging thugs appear with each subsequent level. Some of them jump kick, others point their noggins toward Homer and charge in for a headbutt, and then of course there's a guy who just throws a boomerang. Introduction of new thugs is steadily paced and allows for a gradual learning curve in defending against each new type of attack. In addition to common thugs, the game has a much greater variety of bosses. The cast are all a little less interesting than those wild randos introduced in 1991, but the mechanics to defeat them are also more varied. The first level sees the Mayor of Springfield calling in thugs while he hides in the trunk of his limo, forcing the player to wait until they can drag him out of the trunk while still defending against common thugs that continually stream in. Each level also introduces both a mid-level boss and a final boss, effectively doubling the number of such encounters when compared to the original game. The characters playing the roles of bosses are across the spectrum of Springfield's beloved regulars, from the Squeaky-Voiced Teen as a mall employee to the Rich Texan as the head of the GOP Headquarters, all before finally encountering both Smithers and Mr. Burns as the expected final duo. It's a fun bunch alright.

Cashing in the spousal assist token.

The levels themselves are not as vibrant as one would hope, lacking the little touches like animals and background characters that were integral to the charm of Konami's beat 'em up. However they are very much derived from locales and story elements that developed over the course of the nearly two decades of the television show available in 2009. The first level is the bog standard Downtown Springfield from nearly every *Simpsons* game ever made, but they then branch out into new and different locations. There's the Springfield Mall, GOP Headquarters (my personal favorite), and Channel 6 Studios among them. All together there are six fully fleshed out levels, two less than the original, however they are all generally longer and the mid-level boss fights introduce some extra fleshiness that makes the overall level of content less of a concern. In fact, a full playthrough of the mobile version of the game is longer than the original arcade game.

Overall, there's just a bit of polish that's missing from this version of the game. Latter-day *Simpsons* games always show when they've had professional animation and visual support, and this game doesn't look like one of the games that got such support. It's okay but could've been better. Audio is bare and there are only a few sound bites scattered throughout the game, with none of the dialogue receiving any voice acting. It surely made the game cheaper to produce, but also makes it feel a bit lacking.

Republicans? Let me at 'em!

It wasn't just the iPhone that saw this game grace its App Store. EA Mobile and IronMonkey created crunched down versions of the game for Java and Blackberry feature phones that featured more old school pixel art and pared down boss encounters. The art does have a certain charm to it, but overall the game just looks simpler and even more barren than the already dumbed down designs of the iPhone version. They kept all the levels and generally the same gameplay, but Homer could no longer jump, which is a crucial feature that is sorely missing when certain enemies gain the ability to stun lock the player if they can't jump out of a corner. It's a decent effort for the reduced capabilities of the limited hardware, but the iPhone version (perhaps played on an iPad) is absolutely where it's at if someone has to play this game.

The burden of history weighs heavily.

The Simpsons Arcade for mobile was a good attempt at keeping the license relevant among casual players, but it just lacked the replayability that would make it a memorable game for the hardcore set. That forgettable gameplay (coupled with the game's disappearance from digital stores just two years later due to compatibility issues) means the game just didn't have a chance at sticking around. Now, it's only a few curious folks who search for the game on YouTube that show any interest in the game's existence. And, of course, your humble *Simpsons* video game archivist.

Chapter 25: The Monkey's Paw

The Simpsons Tapped Out - March 2012

I've worked in video games for a while, and what I'm going to write next is probably the result of a career spent mostly in the world of traditional video game products. The way of things was make a game, release a game, be done with the game. That's how I like to work and that's the kind of game I personally like to play. I had a few brushes with working on so-called service games, such as the *Sims* series in which a base game is released and expansion packs follow for years and years. I knew immediately that I had to get out of that. The model in which a game becomes a service or platform—constantly fed a steady stream of content and features—is about the last thing I want to be a part of. And as far as playing those games, when does it end? I need it to end.

My annual October ritual.

You know who doesn't want it to end? Companies that want to make lots and lots of money. It's like opening a spigot of cash and putting in all the resources to make sure it flows on for years and years. The aforementioned expansion pack model worked in the age of physical products, but the App Store age introduced the possibility of milking players through a little something called microtransactions. This model allows a company to release a game for free so that anyone can download and play it, but through careful monetization design, they can encourage players to spend real money to gain access to features that make the game more playable and, well, fun.

This freemium model became the next jewel in EA Mobile's eye. As we've already seen, EA spent several years beefing up their mobile division, both by bolstering their internal staff and buying up development studios with proven track records in the mobile space. Though they'd released three mobile games by the end of 2009, EA Mobile probably didn't see much revenue from them. After all, paying five bucks for a two hour experience probably wasn't a best-selling idea.

And so they went back to the drawing board. The question was how do they make a *Simpsons* mobile game that turns into money but also has the high quality expected of a game based on *The Simpsons?* They turned to a style of game called a "clicker," or in the case of mobile, a tapper game. The game doesn't require swipes or moving characters around. The player simply taps. Tap menus, tap characters, tap whatever shiny animated thing is calling their attention. This formed the foundation of an idea that EA Mobile brought to the folks at Fox. According to producers from the show, it was a studio called Bight Games that brought the idea to them.[1]

Lisa's going to read The Bridges of SADison County, eh? Eh?
Bah whatever, it's the final chapter.

Like the last several companies we've seen in this book, Bight Games started their existence as a mobile game studio. They weren't independent for long before EA Mobile scooped them up as well in August 2011. As part of EA Mobile, they suggested using the *Simpsons* license to make a game in which players must not just explore Springfield, but build it out themselves. The idea caught on with the folks at Fox, who themselves were well familiar with the variety of freemium games available on their smartphones. I wouldn't be surprised if it was the first time a game pitch instantly caught on with the staff of the television show, seeing as everyone had a smartphone by 2011 and there was no shortage of simple tapper games on the App Store.

And that is where the idea for *The Simpsons Tapped Out* originated. It launched in March 2012 and was so popular out of the gate that the servers crashed, leaving many unhappy fans in the first few months. It took some time to stabilize, but the developers eventually found their footing. Eight years and two hundred million dollars later, there's so much content for the game that it can't possibly all be experienced... at least not without spending thousands of real dollars to speed things along.[2]

Choose your time sink.

Matt Selman—executive producer of the show—has the best introduction for the game: "The essence of *Tapped Out* has been, 'How can we insult *Tapped Out* as much as we can?'"[3]

While we'd finally seen a dedicated writing crew from the *Simpsons* staff for *The Simpsons Game*, there hadn't been much need for writing on the mobile games. None of them were story-heavy and the few bits of text and dialogue had the kinds of jokes I might write in two minutes on a bus, so the games didn't feel like a professional writer spent time drafting the perfect way to explain how to make Homer jump on landmines. With *Tapped Out*, several writers from the *Simpsons* staff dedicate their time to actually craft all of the dialogue in the game. The dialogue isn't voiced (which would be prohibitively expensive with the amount of dialogue in this game), but there's enough sound and small voice clips from the archive to keep things aurally interesting. This leads to the design philosophy outlined above in which the fourth wall is constantly broken and no punches are pulled in making fun of players for playing such a dumb game. But it was the kind of dumb that many of us have fallen into in our game-playing lives. J. Stewart Burns, writer from the show and head writer for *Tapped Out*, noted that "EA got a little annoyed at first. They didn't really like the idea that we were insulting people as they were spending money in the game and calling them idiots for that."[4] After all, a free game is a free game and not a bad way to pass some time during a commute. Eventually, it's easy to see how a game with a steady drip feed of jokes can entice players to spend real money to get faster access to the comedy.

But beyond the character dialogue is the actual gameplay. The premise sets up the idea that Springfield has blown up and it's up to Homer and the player (characterized as a giant sky finger) to rebuild the town by completing quests and earning new buildings, props, and characters to expand the town. The Simpson house is the first available building but additional structures and their associated characters are unlocked as quests are completed. A quest is simply a time sink in which a character is directed to perform a task, such as planting a tomacco field, which is automatically completed after a certain amount of time. Therein lies the bait. A player can decide to grind it out and simply wait for those tasks to complete, or they can spend the game's virtual currency to instantly complete the task. Donuts are the currency used for accelerating tasks and while some donuts can be earned through gameplay, they are as rare as penguins in the tropics. But hey, there's a virtual store right there. Why not spend some real dough to get a few more donuts? I know I did when I first played. I justified it based on the fact that I'd played a certain number of hours, so why not kick them a few real bucks? There's also an in-game cash currency that can be used to buy some buildings and items, but the prime content always requires donuts.

I think it would look better two pixels to the left.

Beyond that predatory monetization stuff, there's actually a fun little game. The genre for this sort of thing is called a city builder, because that's basically what the player is doing the entire time. Stuck in an isometric perspective, the player can move their camera around the map and place buildings and props as they unlock them. For proper city planners, it all begins with roads and paths to lay out the grid for their Springfield, and then buildings are placed. The diehard fans try to match the layout seen in the real Springfield (such as it is), but players are allowed to get as wacky as they please. Fulfill Homer's dream by placing Moe's Tavern and the Kwik-E-Mart next to the Simpson house. Move over to Krustyland and build the deadly theme park of your dreams. Forget Springfield altogether and build the perfect Halloween town, as I did. The sheer amount of content is staggering and players will never run out of new things to place in their town. Space is limited, so eventually players must also buy additional land to expand their town. A classic lesson in real estate development.

My playing curve just about matched that description. I resisted the game for years because, as I already said, I need things to end. But I couldn't be an avid *Simpsons* game guy and not play it, so I eventually gave in and checked out the game. I built the town as accurately as I could get it, using sources such as the map in *Virtual Springfield*[5] (Chapter 14) and the hyper-detailed Springfield map by Jerry Lerma and Terry Hogan.[6] And, you know, that was fun for a while. I spent that bit of money on donuts and that helped me get a few more cool things. I was drawn to the "Treehouse of Horror" content, of course. But eventually I found myself wanting more and I was sure as heck no whale. That, dear reader, is when I cheated and cheated hard. I was playing the Android OS version and found a handy hacked app of the game that allowed me to grant myself a ridiculous amount of cash and donuts, which in turn allowed me to expand the size of the map and acquire more buildings than I knew what to do with. This fast track to the late game content did allow me to add some cool stuff to my Springfield, but it also led me to the point where the game just wasn't interesting anymore. I had a town of Springfield folks, aliens walking alongside the kids from Springfield Elementary. It was a wild west of jokes and characters, but

the chaos wasn't enough to sustain my interest. I needed
it to end, and I ended it.

Spend, my pretties, spend!

I check in now and then as new expansions are
released, but I usually only download the "Treehouse of
Horror" stuff around Halloween time. During those
annual visits to my town, I find myself wondering about
the legacy of this game. It won't go on forever, right? I
can't imagine. It's sad to think that the servers may
someday get shut down and the game just... won't exist
anymore. I dream of a version of this game, when all is
said and done, in which all the content is packaged up into
a single app. No online connection, none of those service
features. Just a standalone city builder, you know? The
Springfield version of *Sim City*. It may work or may not,
but if you lock a hundred game designers in a room for a
hundred years, I'm sure they can do it. They can take

some of those hundreds of millions of dollars and make it happen.

Doesn't everyone have a "Treehouse of Horror" village?

But until then, *The Simpsons Tapped Out* is the only game in town. It's been in development for eight years and earned so much money that I can't see EA ever deciding to try anything else. In many ways, this game ticks the boxes I've outlined as requirements for a good *Simpsons* game. The stories are driven by the writers from the show, and the dialogue is straight from their brains. It's so self-aware and jokey with its video game existence that even the most dense player can recognize when they're being made fun of. The jokes are so jam-packed in there that players barely have time to breathe. The art isn't the janky 3D goofballs that horrified us in the early aughts. All of the art and animation is on par with anything one might see on the television show (if all the action was only seen from one angle). So, you know, it's got good stuff! It's maybe all we could have hoped for.

And maybe, just maybe, this is the *Simpsons* video game that we deserve.

Notes

1. "The Simpsons: 30 Years of Video Games and Jokes About Video Games" (YouTube, 2019). Archived by gameslice on youtube.com. Retrieved 21 March 2021.

2. "Waleed Kamel" (Linkedin, 2014). Retrieved 21 March 2021.

3. "The Simpsons: 30 Years of Video Games and Jokes About Video Games."

4. Ibid.

5. "The Simpsons: Virtual Springfield - City Map" (GameFAQs, 2005). Modified and archived on gamefaqs.com. Retrieved 21 March 2021.

6. "Guide to Springfield USA by Jerry Lerma and Terry Hogan" (reddit, 2018). Archived by Ender_Skywalker on reddit.com. Retrieved 21 March 2021.

Acknowledgements: The Gratitude

I can trace the genesis of this project back to when I began listening to the *Talking Simpsons* podcast hosted by Bob Mackey, Henry Gilbert, and Chris Antista, which led me to the *Retronauts* podcast hosted by the aforementioned Bob Mackey and Jeremy Parish. Between the shot of *Simpsons* nostalgia and the retro video game booster, I couldn't help but dig into my own video game origins. In addition, Jeremy Parish has created a fantastic series of videos and anthology books under the *Video Works* umbrella which documents every video game ever released, in chronological order, and on a variety of platforms. Jeremy's work was my single biggest inspiration for writing this book and anyone interested in video game history would do well to check out his work.

I am a wimp and did not personally interview anyone for this book, but my research revealed a wealth of information and interviews that helped me to piece together the stories of the video games in this book. Thank you to these writers, archivists, researchers, and all-around cool ~~nerds~~ enthusiasts for their valuable research and resources: Aaron Bleyaert, Aaron Demeter, Al Backiel, Blake J. Harris, Bob Mackey, Brendan Sinclair, bubufubu, Chloe Albanesius, Chris Antista, Chris Turner, Colou, Dan Ackerman, David Adams, Donut Team, Ender_Skywalker, Eurogamer, GameFAQs, gameslice,

Hans Reutter, Hari Kondabolu, Henry Gilbert, Imoyoshi, Indie Gamer Chick, Jack Yarwood, James Kinsella, Jeremy Parish, Jerry Lerma, John Ortved, Liam Robertson, Lizzie Crocker, Madeline Berger, Michael Melamedoff, Miyabi, Morgan Kuno, NintendoComplete, Peter Barnard, Sami, Sarah Marsh, Simpsons Wiki, Sketch the Cow, Terry Hogan, The Cutting Room Floor, The New York Times, Tokyo Fox, T.S., Wendy Jackson, and Zach Nagle.

While I did not personally interview them, the following developers and publisher folks that worked on these video games shared valuable insights in other publications that helped to provide more context for the creation of these works: Alex DeMeo, Athena Bax, Carolyn Omine, Dan Kitchen, David Crane, Garry Kitchen, Jeff Westbrook, Joe McGinn, Kamio-san, Matt Selman, Michael Ebert, Michael Viner, Paul Provenzano, Rob LaZebnik, Stewart Burns, Takeuchi-san, and Waleed Kamel.

Thanks to all the beloved boarders at GameFAQs, NoHomers, Maggied, and shiftercar for stoking the embers of this low-key nerdom for all those turbulent years when I might've spent my time on more valuable hobbies and pursuits. I've also worked in video games for nearly two decades and am so grateful to all my friends and coworkers from my time at Vivendi Universal Games, Electronic Arts, Experis, and Double Fine Productions with whom I shared some of the most wonderful, stressful, and fulfilling moments of my career. Finally, I owe my continued attempts at writing to the many gifted writers whose work I had the good fortune to read and from whom I learned so much, including those who I met at GameFAQs, SMCCD, Tumblr, and Everything2.

Rob, thanks for letting me ditch *The Sims* to go work on *The Simpsons Game*!

I will never forget the early influences of writer Wilson Lau and webmaster Simon Lau (no relation) for inspiring me to contribute giant documents about video games to the Internet.

And last but not least, thanks to Abe, Edith, Maddie, Kelly, Abby, Henry, Cris, Alex, Maggi, Mom, and Pop for their unending support and patience with... all this. *waves hands around*

www.ingramcontent.com/pod-product-compliance
Lightning Source LLC
LaVergne TN
LVHW022333060326
832902LV00022B/4014